French Dolls

In Color

Third Series

Patricia R. Smith

French Dolls

In Color

Third Series

Patricia R. Smith

COLLECTOR BOOKS
P.O. Box 3009
Paducah, KY 42001

The current values in this book should be used only as a guide. They are not intended to set prices, which vary from one section of the country to another. Auction prices as well as dealer prices vary greatly and are affected by condition as well as demand. Neither the Author nor the Publisher assumes responsibility for any losses that might be incurred as a result of consulting this guide.

Additional copies of this book may be ordered from:

COLLECTOR BOOKS
P.O. Box 3009
Paducah, Kentucky 42001

@$14.95. Add $2.00 for postage and handling.

Printed and bound in Singapore by Singapore National Printers Ltd. through Four Colour Imports, Ltd., Louisville, Kentucky.

Contents

Credits

THANK YOU to all the collectors that have helped with all our books, and a special thank you to the following for the use of their dolls in this volume:

Kitty Best
Irene Brown
Joanna Brunken
Elizabeth Burke
Marlowe Cooper
Rosalind Cranor
Helen Draves
Barbara Earnshaw-Cain
Jo Fasnacht
Frashers Doll Auctions
(Rt. 1, Box 72, Oak Grove, MO. 64075)
Shirlie Glass
O.D. Gregg
Jeanne Haskins
Pauline Hoch
Kimport Dolls
Florence Main
Jay Minter
Penny Pendlebury
Marion & Elsie Reins
Ethel Stewert
Pat Timmons
Cathy Turchan
Turn of Century Antiques
(1415 S. Broadway, Denver, CO. 80220)
Burnice Wallen
Kathy Walters
Lori Weston
Josephine Wingfield
Carol & Elliot Zirlin
(Hobby Horse Doll Shop, Dallas, TX)

Foreword

We are often asked in what order, if a list were to be made, would the rareness of French dolls line up. The following list is based on availability of doll for sale:

A. Marque
200 Series Jumeau (incised)
B.M. (Mothereau)
H.G. (Guimonneau)
A.T.
H.
French Court Dolls
Huret Child or Fashion
Rohmer
S.F.B.J. rare 200 series characters
B.F. (Bébé Francais)
R.D.
E.D.
Schmitt & Fils
Bébé Gesland

Jullien
Phenix Bébé
Mascotte
Paris Bébé
Mechanicals
All Bisque
Bru
Steiner, Jules
Eden Bébé
Belton-Types
Jumeau
Fashions
F.G.
DEP.
Limoges
Unis
S.F.B.J.

Doll rarity is not based on the prices paid for them, but on the desirability and how many are ever for sale. There would be an entirely different listing if it were based on prices paid!

Pricing in general is difficult, but the determining factor in pricing a bisque doll is the head and that it is on the correct body. The quality of the bisque is extremely important, and the best bisque is flawless in the "depth" of the bisque—that is the look of the bisque, not the actual thickness. There must be no damage to the head which would include even a slight, small hairline crack, cracked or broken shoulderplates, eye chips or cracks, nor any mends or repairs and even a chip of a pierced ear may play a part in the price.

The most desirable dolls would be ones that are completely perfect, in original clothes, with original box, plus never having been played with. BUT, this is very unrealistic as the ratio is an overwhelming 6000 to 1 against finding a doll in even part of the above stated condition (original clothes or in original box). That leaves many, many dolls showing various degrees of use—so prices in books are based on perfect dolls with excellent quality bisque that has no defects. Occasionally there are flecks that look like dirt in the bisque of a fine doll, and the majority of collectors will not purchase these dolls unless they are priced far below the asking price for a perfect example. Some collectors may find that if there are just a very few flecks, and they do not find them distracting that they can purchase a high quality doll at a very fair price.

Body rubs, a missing finger, a crack in a kid body, a minor repair to the foot, etc. are minor, not major damages and the only part they should play in the prices of the dolls is small.

There are some French dolls that have characteristics unique to a certain maker, such as a Bru body, a Steiner, or a typical Jumeau body and with a little study, a collector can become familiar with these differences and be able to recognize if the head is on the correct body. One point is important in regards to bodies and that is that the German makers loved to put in knee detail, such as dimples and rolls, where the French makers ran the upper leg flat into the lower leg without any knee detail. Most French bodies have legs that are jointed at the knees, but are flush jointed, and the Germans generally had a space between the upper and lower leg at the knee joint. Another point is about heads, the Germans loved to make double chins where the majority French enjoyed designing dolls with flat, unrolled chins.

In considering prices it must also be considered that collectors set their own prices by what they are willing to pay to get a certain doll, some will certainly pay more than others, and mostly depends on the income of that collector. The collector still buys from dealers, but many have turned to auctions for buying and at this moment are willing to pay high prices to get the dolls they want. The prices of French dolls have continued to rise and will continue to do so, but as the prices go higher the collector becomes much more discriminating and is demanding the best for the money. A perfect, rare or not so rare French (or any other) doll that is unique in being in original clothes, having an original box and being in extremely fine condition will sell well over any book value and be worth that amount of money as the super fine example of any doll is so rare!

All Bisque Dolls

French all bisque dolls are rather rare when compared with how many can be found that were made in Germany and Japan. We feel what has added to their rarity is the fact that there are very few French all bisque that are authenticated.

French all bisque dolls have a swivel head, generally are peg strung with kid lined joints so the bisque does not squeek, nor chip around the joints so easily.

The swivel heads on French dolls generally are molded with a loop at the base of the neck. The loops are easily identified as they look like the top of bells:

In the small sizes the eyes are usually set and are generally blue with no pupil, but as the dolls get larger they gain pupils and sleep.

French legs are much more varied than the German made ones. They were mainly made barefooted, are thinner and much more delicate than the German made dolls. There are many that do have vertical, as well as, circular ribbed stockings in many colors that include white, blue, brown, black and yellow. If they have molded-on shoes, some may be high-top boots with pointed toes or high buttoned ones with four or more painted straps. They may have brown, pink, blue or black one- or two-strap slippers with or without heels and some may have bows. They may also have stockings that are painted to the hips.

The French-made all-bisque dolls will have good quality painted flesh tones and are artistically done. They generally have open crowns with tiny cork pates, and the detail work by the artist for the eyelashes, mouth and the multistroke painted eye brows are excellent. A few very rare French all bisque dolls will also be jointed at the elbows and knees. It should be added that French all bisque rarely have an open mouth.

Plate 1. 3¾″ with bisque heads, painted features and on composition bodies and marked on back of heads: 71 Unis France 149 301. Each doll is original, and each has a red string attached to the head for hanging. It is reasonable to assume they were Christmas tree ornaments, as the girl carries a candy cane over one arm. Courtesy Rosalind Cranor.

Plate 2. 6″ called "The French Wrestler" due to the modeling of the fat and muscled legs. These dolls may have bare feet or have painted-on high-top boots. Swivel head, closed mouth and glass eyes. Pristine mint in original clothes. Courtesy Shirlie Glass.

A.T.

A. Thuillier made dolls in Paris from 1875 to 1893 and may be the makers of the A.T. marked dolls. The A.T. marked dolls have been found on wooden, composition with straight wrists or jointed wrists, and kid bodies, and it is known that A. Thuillier made dolls in these combinations. The A.T. marked dolls can have a full closed mouth or an open mouth with two rows of teeth. They made and sold dolls that were undressed as well as the fully dressed ones and the dolls can range from size 12″ up to 30″.

The quality of A.T. marked dolls generally are breathtaking for any collector who loves French dolls, but they can also be of moderate or "late, with heavy color," where the quality is not too good. Collectors must remember that only the finest dolls command the prices that will be quoted. They must have excellent quality bisque and be on the correct wooden and composition or kid body to command the high prices placed on these scarce dolls.

The dolls will be marked with an A., followed by a size number, then a T, or they can be marked with the A.T., followed by No. 6, etc. The A.T. mark is found extremely high on the back of the bisque head.

As far as beauty, these dolls usually will outclass any other French doll that is placed around them. They have a common look among themselves that once seen and studied makes it easy to pick one out of a crowd of French dolls. Because of the beauty they have always commanded high prices for the times, for example in the 1960's a marked A.T of 24″ would cost $850.00-1,000.00, and that was almost 30 years ago.

Plate 3. 15″ A 5 T. incised high on head. The ears are pierced and applied. The mouth is closed with white line between lips. Original mache body with unjointed wrists. Wears original A.T. marked slippers. Courtesy Marlowe Cooper. Photo by Don Allen.

Plate 4. 23½″ marked: A 9 T. Has open mouth with two rows of teeth, very dark paperweight eyes, and is on jointed composition body. Very old clothes. Courtesy Kimport Dolls.

Belton-Types

It is highly unlikely that "Belton" dolls is a correct term, even "Belton-types" do not really do them justice from the standpoint of the time in history when Belton was active. If you read the following you will see why.

Belton is listed as a doll maker from 1842 to 1846, then Belton and Jumeau are listed together from 1847 to 1852, then nothing until the Widow Belton is listed from 1856 to 1857. It is very doubtful that these bisque headed dolls could have been made as early as the dates shown above. We do know that Belton and Jumeau received an honorable mention at the 1844 Paris Exposition, but it is not known for what item.

The Belton story begins in 1842 and ends in 1857 as an F. Pottier is named the successor to the Widow Belton's business. We have a mystery at the beginning and the end, as we have no information as to who F. Pottier was. This added to the mystery of the middle where we have no information and it all adds up to nothing.

Why the word "Belton" ever became attached to a certain style doll is not known and may never be known. What is known is that "Belton-type" dolls have been accepted as being French and run into a certain price range.

Plate 5. 20″ Belton-type with concave top to head and three holes. Open/closed mouth with white area between lips. Jointed body with straight wrists. Courtesy Jay Minter.

So-called Belton dolls have a saucer, or concave top to the head that is solid bisque (with no crown cut). These dolls will have two or three holes. Two of the holes are used for stringing the doll and if a third hole is present, it was used for plugging the doll's wig to the top of the head.

"Dome heads" or "Bald heads" are different and most of German origin. The German heads are solid shaped and completely round on top, although some may have holes in these round domes for stringing, or three holes with the third being used for plugging the wig. It would be a fair assumption that all Belton-types were actually made in Germany.

Belton-type dolls have almost white bisque, have open/closed mouths (some may have a full closed mouth) with the area between the lips left white. They will generally have a pink wash over the eyes and will be on a French body.

Markings on the Belton-type dolls are size number only or some will have a mold number along with the size number. (For example 116, 120, 127, 136, 183, 190, 224, etc.)

Plate 6. 21″ Belton-type socket head on jointed body with straight wrists. Open/closed mouth with white area between lips. Concave top to head with two holes for stringing. Ears are pierced into head. Marks: 14, on head.

Plate 7. 13″ Belton-type doll with concave top to head and two holes, original skin wig, close closed mouth, pierced ears and on French body with straight wrists. Very old costume maybe original. Marks: 137. Courtesy Frasher Auctions.

Plate 8. 14½″ Belton-type with concave top to head and three holes for stringing and wig. Closed mouth and is marked: 5, on the head. Composition jointed body. Courtesy Kimport Dolls.

Plate 9. 12″ Socket head on French composition body with straight wrists. Paperweight eyes and open/closed mouth with white area between lips. All original clothes except necklace. Concave top to head with three holes. Marks: 137/3. Courtesy Helen Draves.

Plate 10. 11½″ Belton-type with excellent quality bisque. Open/closed mouth, pierced ears and has two holes on top of head for stringing. Lathe turned inside and out, wood body, papier mache arms and legs with wooden dowel pins. Ears pierced into head. Painted on orange hose with five-strap boots.

Plate 11. 20″ Belton-type with concave top to head and has two holes for stringing. Wide open/closed mouth with area between lips left white. Straight wrists, jointed French body.

Plate 12. 12″ Belton-type with open/closed mouth and white area between lips. On jointed body with straight wrists. Ears pierced into head. Courtesy Jay Minter.

Plate 13. 14½″ Belton-type with concave head and three holes. Two used for stringing and other for "plugging" of original wig. Closed mouth and set eyes. Courtesy Jay Minter.

B.F.

B.F. marked dolls have been found in original Bébé Francais boxes, and the trademark for Bébé Francais was used by Danel & Cie (after 1891), Jumeau (1896) and S.F.B.J. (after 1899).

B.F. marked dolls can be excellent to medium quality in artists workmanship, but the bisque is generally excellent. They will come on French jointed composition bodies with straight wrists (some will have jointed wrists), closed mouth and have pierced ears. There will be a size number between the two letters, for example: B. 6 F.

Plate 14. 15″ Marked: B. 6. F. ca. 1875. Closed mouth, very short upper arms on jointed composition body and has straight wrists.

Plate 15. 20″ Marked: B.F. on head. Heavy feathered eyebrows, closed mouth and pierced ears. On jointed French body with straight wrists.

Bru

The founders of this company were Leon Casimir Bru and his wife. Between 1867 and 1869 they took out several French patents that included "The Surprise Doll," a double faced doll. Madame Bru patented another in 1872 made of wood and metal that contained a multi disc music box. Earlier they had patented a crying doll, and in 1869 they patented a new doll body made with ball joints and included joints at the wrists, ankles and waist, one of all papier mache and white kid. They also worked in rubber, porcelain, "hardened paste," and carved wooden joints.

Casimir Bru, Jeune (junior) started or continued the company under the name Bru Jne & Cie (Bru Junior & Co.) about 1873 as he is listed on several patents between 1873 and 1882. These patents included a jointed rubber doll (1878) which was built over a wire frame, a nursing doll (Bébé Teteur-1879), and a kid bodied doll (1879), the movements of eyelids while the eyes would remain stationary (1882) and one interesting patent—for a boat that was mechanical with the patent in the name of Bru & Jumeau. (1882).

Advertisements for Bru Jne & Cie between 1873 and 1883 show dolls in carved wood (hands and feet), dolls with music boxes, dolls in "ordinary wood" with simple joints, rubber dolls, dolls in kid with arms and hands in jointed wood, two faced dolls with one side asleep and the other awake, kid bodied dolls with rubber heads, mechanical talking dolls (1879) and the eating Bébé Gourmand in 1881.

As for exhibits at International shows, Bru Jne & Cie exhibited in Paris in 1878 and received a silver medal, in 1880 they were at Melbourne and also received a silver medal. Apparently Bru dolls did not receive any gold medals until the time of H. Chevro (1883).

In 1883, when H. Chevrot took over the Bru firm he retained the name Bru. That same year he took out a patent for a kid body doll with a system of joints manipulated from the interior of the doll. From 1883 to 1889 he continued making dolls with newer patented joints, the Bébé Teteur (nursing doll), Bébé Gourmand (eating doll) and the new Bébé Le Dormeur (sleeping by means of eyelids).

The factory at Montreuill-Sous-Bois made the bisque heads, and an ad in 1885 states "The words Bébé Bru can be examined on each Bébé," which would mean chest labels as well as the incised marks.

All the gold medals won by Bru were under H. Chevrot ownership. 1885, Paris and Antwerp, 1886 Liverpool and Paris, 1887 LeHavre and Toulouse, 1888 gold and silver medals were awarded the firm and these expositions were held at Barcelona, Melbourne and Paris. They continued to win gold medals in 1889 at Paris, 1893 at Chicago and so it may be stated that the "golden years" of the Bru firm were under the direction of H. Chevrot.

From 1890 to 1899 the Bru firm moved into the hands of Paul Eugene Girard. He continued to patent new ideas like the combination of movement of eyes and eyelids (standard sleep eyes), a walking and talking doll that had a key wind mechanism and was called Bébé Petit Pas, a Mama-Papa doll with expanding chest (1892). Also patented were kissing dolls that threw kisses as a string was pulled (1885), and a doll that threw kisses by leg movement and also walked and talked, this one patented by Paul Girard's son, Eugene Fredrick Girard in 1897, dolls with hollow wooden bodies, composition heads and natural eyelashes. As late as 1892 they were still making India rubber dolls and the Bébé Teteur as late as 1898.

After 1899, the Bru firm evolved into part of the Société Francaise de Fabrication de Bébés Jouets (S.F.B.J.).

As to marks and dates for Bru dolls, the Bébé Brevete was made in the 1870's and will have a size number on head and an oval sticker on chest: Bébé Brevete S.G.D.G. Paris and will have an all kid body with bisque lower arms and closed mouth.

Circle Dot Bébés were made in the 1870's and will be marked ⊙ ◠ with some also incised Bru Jne. They will have all kid bodies with bisque lower arms and closed mouths. The area in back of the head that is incised with the ⊙ ◠ is in the exact same position as the cut out area for the Bébé Teteur (nursing doll).

The Bébé Teteur-Nursing Bru was made from 1878 to 1898 and had a kid body with upper arms and legs of metal covered with kid and lower legs of carved wood. They can also be on jointed composition bodies. The mouth is open with a hole for the nipple from a bottle. There is a rubber ball inside the head and a metal wire that protrudes from the back of the head, and when turned causes the bulb to deflate then inflate to bring the liquid from the baby bottle into and back out of the head so the doll has the appearance of nursing.

Bru Jne Bébé was mostly made in the 1880's. It had a closed mouth, kid body, bisque, lower arms, kid over wood upper arms with hinged elbows, and wooden lower legs which also had kid over wood upper legs, or full wooden legs.

The Bru Jne R Bébé was made in the early 1890's with excellent quality bisque, and an open mouth. It has a jointed composition body that is stamped Bébé Bru and size number. Head will be incised Bru Jne R and size number.

Plate 16. 21″ Bru. This doll is totally original in wig and clothes and has open/closed mouth with molded teeth barely showing, pierced ears, kid body with bisque lower arms and is marked: incised circle and dot on back of head and Bru Jne 7 on shoulder plate. Courtesy Frasher Auctions.

Plate 17. Close up of Circle Dot Bru with open/closed mouth. Courtesy Frasher Auctions.

Plate 18. 20″ Circle Dot Bru (marked with ⊙ on back of head). Has large paperweight eyes, open/closed mouth, pierced ears and original caracul wig. Swivel head on shoulder plate, kid body with bisque lower arms. Molded breasts on shoulder plate. Courtesy of Turn of Century Antiques.

Plate 19. Shows the side view of Circle Dot Bru so the molded breasts can be seen. Courtesy of Turn of Century Antiques.

Plate 20. 20″ Bru Brevette with paper sticker on chest. Kid body with bisque lower arms. May be original clothes. Open/closed mouth and excellent quality bisque. Courtesy Kimport Dolls.

Plate 21. 22½″ Marked Bru Brevette with paper sticker on chest. Bisque head on bisque shoulder plate. Kid body with bisque lower arms. Replaced clothes. Courtesy Kimport Dolls.

Plate 22. Close up of lovely Bru Brevette with sticker on chest. Closed mouth and swivel socket head on bisque shoulder plate. Courtesy Kimport Dolls.

Plate 23. 20″ "Bébé Teteur" open mouth/nurser of 1879. Full kid body with bisque lower arms. Marks: Bru/Jne/8, on head and Bebe Bru/No 8 on shoulder plate. Original wig. Courtesy Barbara Earnshaw-Cain.

Plate 24. 17″ Bisque socket head on bisque shoulder plate. Kid over wood body with bisque lower arms and wood lower legs. Open/closed mouth, pierced ears and all original clothes. Replaced wig. Marks: Bru Jne, on head. Bru Jne 5 and No. 5 over edge of shoulder plate. Shoes marked: Bru Jne/Paris, in oval.

Plate 25. 19″ Marked Bru Jne 7 on head and shoulder plate. Kid body, bisque lower arms and wooden lower legs. Pierced ears. Human hair wig and original clothes. Courtesy O.D. Gregg.

Plate 26. 17″ Bru Jne. Has bisque swivel head on bisque shoulder plate with molded breasts, closed mouth and paperweight eyes. Gusseted kid body with scalloped edge at shoulder plate, kid over wood upper arms, bisque lower arms and wooden lower legs. Hinge joints at elbows and knees. Original clothes and wig. Courtesy Ethel Stewart.

Plate 27. 30″ Bru twins marked: Bru Jne R 13 on heads. Jointed composition bodies with very unusual hands that are curved. Original clothes. Courtesy Barbara Earnshaw-Cain.

Plate 28. 14″ Marked: Bru Jne /5 on head and shoulder. Swivel head on bisque shoulder plate, all kid body with bisque lower arms. Pierced ears and stitched toes.

Plate 29. 21″ Socket head on jointed composition and wood body. Marks: Bru Jne R/9 on head and has open mouth and pierced ears.

Plate 30. 22″ Marked: Bru Jne 10. 12″ head circumference, pierced ears, cork pate and open/closed mouth with slightly molded tongue. Large paperweight eyes and excellent quality bisque. Courtesy Elizabeth Burke.

Plate 31. 14″ Brown fired-in skin tones Bru Jne with brown all kid body. Black paperweight eyes and typical open/closed Bru Jne mouth. Courtesy Kimport Dolls.

Plate 32. 24¼″ Marked: Bru Jne. Wood lower legs, kid body and kid over wood upper arms with Bru bisque lower arms. Closed mouth and pierced ears. Marked Bru shoes and old, maybe original clothes. Courtesy Kimport Dolls.

Plate 33. 24″ Marked: Bru Jne R. Has open mouth, pierced ears and is on fully-jointed French composition body. Dress may be original and has replaced wig. Courtesy Kimport Dolls.

Plate 34. Close up of open mouth marked: Bru Jne R. Courtesy Kimport Dolls.

Court Doll

Plate 35. 16″ French Court Doll that is all original. Cloth body with wooden limbs with painted-on shoes. Has very extreme bust line with most of bust showing above dress line. Courtesy Barbara Earnshaw-Cain.

Plate 36. Side view of the 16″ French Court Doll to show the extreme of the bust line. Courtesy Barbara Earnshaw-Cain.

Plate 37. Underneath view of lower body and legs of the French Court Doll. The shoes are painted on and the feet are flat. Courtesy Barbara Earnshaw Cain.

DEP.

Many dolls, both French and German, bear the mark DEP. as part of the mold description, but the dolls referred to here are marked DEP. and a size number ONLY and are on French jointed bodies. Some of the bodies will have a Jumeau sticker or stamp and some of the DEP. heads will have artist check marks and Tété Jumeau stamp.

The early DEP. marked dolls will have very fine quality bisque, closed mouths, and the artist work on the face details will be excellent. This style doll will date in the 1880's. The dolls marked DEP. that are from the 1890's to 1900 will still have fine quality bisque, and then the later they become, the higher the color, and less attention will be paid to the face detail by the artists. The later dolls will also have painted lashes below the eyes only and most will have hair lashes above the eyes. The early dolls will have outlined lips and the later ones will not.

It is almost certain that the majority, if not all, the DEP. marked heads were actually made in Germany by either Simon & Halbig or Kestner with Simon and Halbig being the most likely candidate.

Example mark: DEP
10

Plate 38. 27" Marked: DEP. on head and is on Jumeau marked body with oval sticker stating: Bébé Jumeau. The body is jointed, but has straight wrists, pierced ears, large very paperweight eyes and has closed mouth. Original wig, and old clothes and shoes. Head most likely made by Simon and Halbig for the French maker. Note heavy double chin.

Plate 39. 25″ Marked: DEP. On jointed French body with straight wrists. Beautiful bisque and open mouth. Courtesy Jay Minter.

Plate 40. 28″ Marked: DEP/12, along with a "2" in black paint and an "1" in red (both colors fired in). Closed mouth and on jointed body marked: Bébé Jumeau/Diplome d Honneur.

E.D.

The French dolls that are marked with an E.D. are generally accepted to have been made by E. Denamur of Paris between 1885 and 1898. These dolls can range from rather poor quality right up to the finest quality in every aspect. Some of the other French makers who could have made these dolls were Douillet or Decamps. E.D. marked dolls won gold medals in 1890 and 1893.

Plate 41. 17″ Marked: E.D. that is all original and looks very much like an F.G. She has closed mouth with "bee-sting" lips, paperweight eyes and a fully jointed French body. The original ribbon across waist reads: Bébé. Courtesy Barbara Earnshaw-Cain.

Plate 42. 21½" Marked: E.9.D and has red artists marks. Closed mouth, pierced ears and is on French jointed composition body with straight wrists. Courtesy Frasher Auctions.

Plate 43. 14″ Marked: E 4 D/Depose. Paperweight eyes, closed mouth, pierced ears. On jointed French composition body. Has very long painted lashes below the eyes and painted eyebrows that almost meet in the middle. Courtesy Kimport Dolls.

Eden Bébé

The dolls marked with "Eden Bébé" were made by the firm of Fleischmann and Bloedel, founded in 1873. This firm had its origins in Bavaria then opened a branch in Paris from which they advertised the "Bébé" made for export. This company is an example of the trade links between France and Germany despite the racial animosity that was deeply felt by both countries.

Fleischmann & Bloedel obtained patents on such items as new joints for dolls in 1890 and in 1892, and a French patent for a walking doll whose head turned as it walked. In 1894, they received a patent for moving eyelids, walking dolls, and a doll that threw kisses and talked when a button was pressed. These were all French patents and the same year they took out a German patent for a kiss-throwing and talking doll. Also in 1895 they took out a German patent for a moving doll. They became assignees of a patent by Claude Joseph Simonot of Paris for a walking doll whose head turned as it walked.

In 1890, they registered in France "Eden Bébé "and as a trademark in Germany in 1896. "Eden Puppen" was registered in Germany in 1892 and "Bébé Triomphe" in France in 1898.

Fleishmann & Bloedel were one of the first members of the Société Francaise de Fabrication de Bébés et Jouets (S.F.B.J.) in 1899. In fact, Fleishmann was head of S.F.B.J. as World War I began, and since he was an alien in France, his property was sequestered by the French Government, and he was deported back to Germany.

Plate 44. 21″ Marked: Eden Bébé/Paris/7. Made by Fleischmann & Bloedel. Set paperweight eyes, pierced ears and has cork pate. Composition jointed body with straight wrists. Closed, very pronounced lips. Courtesy Elizabeth Burke.

Plate 45. 20″ Marked: Eden Bébé/Paris/8/Depose. Large paperweight eyes and open mouth. On jointed French composition body. Courtesy Barbara Earnshaw-Cain.

Plate 46. 21″ Marked: Eden Bébé/Paris/9 Depose. Jointed body with straight wrists. Open mouth with outlined lips. Pierced ears.

Fashions

The term "Fashion doll" should be restricted to those dolls used for transmitting fashions from shop to customer or from country to country. It would actually limit real Fashions to before the 19th century for with the coming of ladies fashion magazines in about 1775 the need for fashion dolls disappeared. There is an article in the September 1944 Antiques magazine by Imogene Anderson and Ruth Cannon that is titled, "Dolls as Purveyors of Fashion" where it is said that fashion dolls were being sent to America as late as 1826 (documented).

These "adult" style dolls were made by a number of French and German firms from about the 1860's on into the 1930's. Many will be marked with a number only, or have a stamp or sticker on the body which may be that of the maker or the store from which they were sold.

Of all the lady dolls, the most desirable is the Huret and Rohmer. Next in desirability is the fully jointed-articulated wood or blown kid bodied dolls. Some of these dolls will have bisque lower arms and/or legs or metal limbs. The most available appears to be the marked F.G. fashions.

Plate 47. 18" Simonne style fashion with articulated jointing and kid over wood body and limbs with lower three-fourth of the arms being made of bisque. All original and has cobalt blue eyes. Courtesy Barbara Earnshaw-Cain.

Plate 48. 17″ Marked Simmone Fashion Lady with bisque swivel head on bisque shoulder plate, kid body with kid legs, but wood articulated arms and bisque lower arms. Paperweight glass eyes. Courtesy Kimport Dolls.

Plate 49. 13″ Rohmer Fashion Lady with Rohmer stamp on edge of chest. Bisque shoulder head with glass eyes, kid body with china glaze lower arms. Upper arms are kid over wood. Courtesy Kimport Dolls.

Plate 50. 18″ With Schmidt style face and on a J. Terrene body. This style body is jointed with kid over wood torso, upper arms are metal and lower arms are bisque. The doll dates from the late 1860's into the 1870's. She is all original and has won a second and first place ribbon. Courtesy Barbara Earnshaw-Cain.

Plate 51. 18″ Rare fashion with molded bisque shoulder plate with bosom, bisque lower arms and bisque lower legs. Metal under kid upper arms and legs. All original clothes and wig. Made by E. Terrance. Modeling detail of hands and feet is extremely well done with well defined finger and toes and well as nails on hands and feet being outlined. Courtesy Barbara Earnshaw-Cain.

Plate 52

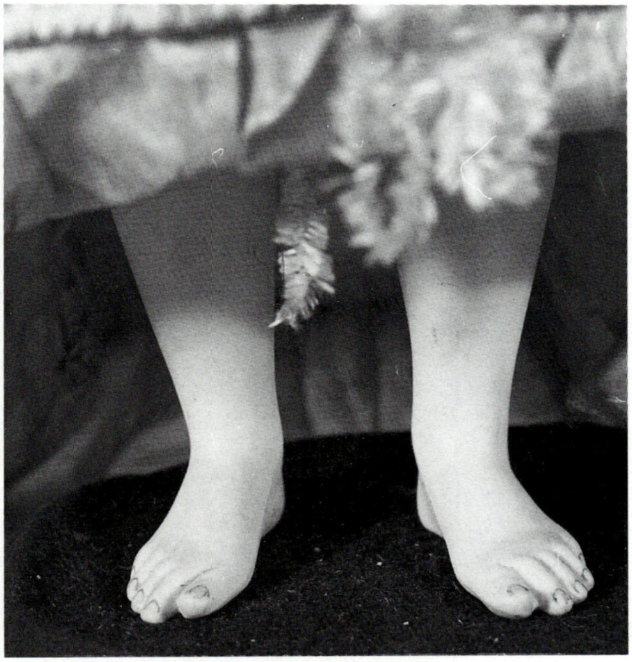

Plate 53

Plate 52-55. 17″ Terrene type fashion with bisque head and shoulder plate and bisque lower arms. Kid body with kid over wood legs. Pierced ears. Courtesy Kimport Dolls.

Plate 54

Plate 55

Plate 56. 18″ Shoulder head, closed mouth and on kid over wood, fully articulated body with the upper body papier mache covered with kid. Marks: E.G./32., which is stamped on the back of the doll's body. Courtesy Jay Minter.

Plate 57. 26″ Fashion with applied ears, swivel neck on bisque shoulder plate. All kid body with leather arms. "Jumeau" stamped in blue on back of body. Portrait style face.

Plate 58. 18″ Jumeau Fashion with socket head on bisque shoulder plate. Lower arms are bisque and upper arms are wood, hinged and covered with kid. Kid body and legs. Marked 2, on head. Courtesy Cathy Turchan.

Plate 59. 15″ Fashion with kid body and bisque lower arms. One piece shoulder and head, glass eyes with black outline around eyes. Marks: Depose E.B. on front shoulder plate. Courtesy Barbara Earnshaw-Cain.

Plate 60. 17½″ Fashion with very pale bisque and has a socket head on bisque shoulder plate, glass eyes with painted lashes, feathered brows and on gusseted kid body with separately stitched fingers. Unmarked. Courtesy Kitty Best.

Plate 61. 13½" "Mona Lisa" Fashion Lady with bisque socket head on bisque shoulder plate. Fully articulated wood body, closed smile mouth and glass eyes. Courtesy Kimport Dolls.

Plate 62. 17" French "smiling" Fashion called "Mona Lisa" by collectors. Head is marked "Depose" on front of the forehead and "F" on back of head. Fully articulated (jointed) wood arms on kid body. Old clothes. Courtesy Barbara Earnshaw-Cain.

Plate 63. 18" Fashion with kid body and bisque lower arms. Bisque socket head on bisque shoulder plate. Marks: F.G. Courtesy Kathy Walters.

Plate 64. 25″ Marked F.G. Fashion Lady with bisque head and shoulder plate. On Gesland stockenette body with bisque hands only. Pink wash over eyes and fully closed mouth. Courtesy Kimport Dolls.

Plate 65. 14″ Huret Fashion Lady with china glaze shoulder head, glass eyes, cork pate and wig. All kid body and limbs. May be original wig, old clothes. Courtesy Kimport Dolls.

Plate 66-67. 14″ Huret Lady with adult features, painted eyes and closed mouth. Very pale bisque, and she is on a fully articulated, all wood body. The hands are very delicate. Marks: Huret, on head. Courtesy Barbara Earnshaw-Cain.

Plate 68. 14″ Huret-type with china glazed head and arms. The body is kid over wood. One piece shoulder and head. Unmarked. Courtesy Barbara Earnshaw-Cain.

Plate 70. Beautiful "Mona Lisa" French Fashion that is now attributed to Bru by some authorities. Bisque socket head on bisque shoulder plate. Kid body with bisque lower arms. Not original clothes. Courtesy Barbara Earnshaw Cain.

Plate 69. 18″ Marked F.G. Fashion with swivel bisque head on bisque shoulder plate. Kid body with bisque lower arms. Slight smile. Original clothes and wig. Courtesy Barbara Earnshaw-Cain.

Plate 71. Unmarked French Fashion on kid body with wired and separated fingers. Original wig, set grey eyes, closed mouth and pierced ears. Bisque swivel shoulder plate and head. Outfit has label of seamstress: Dee Robinson. Courtesy Florence Maine.

Plate 72. 19½″ Early Fashion with one-piece shoulder and head. Outlined dark eyes, on full kid body with bisque lower arms. Original clothes. Courtesy Kimport Dolls.

Plate 73. Close up of the head on the early Fashion. Full closed mouth with dark line between lips. Courtesy Kimport Dolls.

F.G.

Little is known about this company except its initials F.G. There are records of the medals won and atest to the quality of the dolls and clothes. In 1878, they won a silver in Paris, 1880 in Brussels they received a bronze, 1883 a silver in Amsterdam, 1884 a silver in Nice, 1885 a silver in Antwerp, 1889 a silver in Paris and a bronze in Paris in 1900.

F. Gaultier (earlier spelled Gauthier) is the accepted maker of the F.G. marked dolls. These dolls are often found on the cloth covered, or all composition bodies that are marked Gesland. The Gesland Freres (Brothers) firm was operated by two brothers, with one of them having the initials of F.G.

The dolls will be incised on the head: F.G. (inside scroll)

Dolls that are marked with an F. + G. are reproductions that were made in the 1960's in France and are fair to excellent quality, but reproduction prices should be all that is paid for them.

Research done by Florence Poisson, conservator of the Musée Roybet-Fould in Courbevoie, France and published in Bulletin No. 7 (1982) of the Centre D'Etude et de Recherche sur les Poupées in Courbevoie has shown that the founder, Francois Gaultier originally spelled his last name Gauthier and changed the spelling in 1875. His first name as been referred to as Ferdinand or Fernand but Mme. Poisson has shown that the correct first name is Francois.

Plate 74. 30″ Marked: F.G. inside scroll and on fully jointed composition body. Has open mouth with two rows of teeth. The teeth are separate and square on the tops. Courtesy Barbara Earnshaw-Cain.

Plate 75. 15″ Marked: F.G. inside a scroll on head. Closed mouth and all original except wig. Unusual body in that it is all metal and fully jointed.

Plate 76. 21″ Marked: F.G. inside a scroll. Has wooden arms and legs and the body is composition with flaired hips. The hands and feet are papier mache. Closed mouth and pierced ears.

Plate 77. 20″ Marked: F.G., in scroll/8. Socket head on fully jointed French body that is marked: Fque De Bébés Gesland S.D.G.G. along with the Paris address. Has pierced ears and open mouth. Courtesy Frasher Auctions.

Plate 78. 26″ Marked: F.G. in scroll with large paperweight eyes, closed mouth and pierced ears. Very pale bisque and on jointed composition body.

Plate 79. Marked: F.G., in scroll. Closed mouth and large paperweight eyes. On French jointed composition body. Courtesy Kimport Dolls.

Plate 80. 19½″ Marked on head: F.G. inside a scroll. Open mouth and on fully jointed body. Courtesy Barbara Earnshaw-Cain.

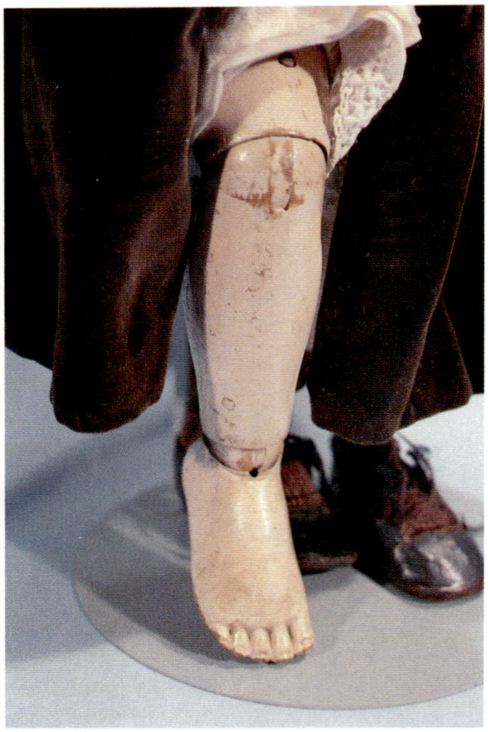

Plate 81 & 82. 21″ Marked: F.G., in scroll. Original coat and hat, shoes and socks. Dress replaced. On all wood body made from boxwood tree. "Pin" jointed body with extra joints at wrists and ankles. Ca. 1878-1880. Some F.G. marked Ladies of Fashion are on same boxwood wooden bodies (only adult figures).

Plate 83. 24″ Marked: F.G., in scroll and has open mouth. Jointed French body and old material clothes. Courtesy Barbara Earnshaw-Cain.

Plate 84. 31″ Bébé Gesland. Body is marked: Bébé A. Gesland, along with two rows of printing that are smudged, but appear to be the address. The body is stockenette covered, and she has composition shoulder plate, lower arms and legs. Bisque head is marked: F.G. in scroll and 11. Closed mouth. Courtesy Frasher Auctions.

Plate 85. 20″ Marked: F.G. in scroll with closed mouth and is on Gesland cloth covered, jointed body with composition lower arms. Courtesy Barbara Earnshaw-Cain.

Plate 86. 28½″. Bébé Gesland with cloth-covered body, composition legs, arms, and shoulder plate. Open mouth with two rows of tiny teeth. Head is marked: F.G. inside a scroll. Body is marked: Gesland.

Plate 87. Bébé Gesland. The body is metal and wood and covered with cloth stockenette. It is jointed and can be posed at the shoulders so the arms will move in any direction.

Plate 88. 29″ Bébé Gesland marked with an F.G. inside a scroll. Large set blue eyes, open mouth with two rows of teeth and very pale bisque. Pierced ears. Courtesy Barbara Earnshaw-Cain.

Fortune Tellers

Fortune Telling dolls are rather a mystery as we have no idea how and when they were used. We do know they were called Oracle dolls are made by the French as well as the Germans. We also know that under the skirt are many slips of paper that are folded so they tuck up and form the "slip" to the outfit. The dolls are dressed as Gypsy Fortune Tellers and the fortunes are hand written on the pages. On some of these dolls the lower torso and limbs are formed from a cardboard cylinder and a few come with their own attached stand.

Plate 89. 18″ tall Fortune Telling Doll that is marked on its bisque swivel head: F.G. The doll is all original and has folded sheets of paper under the skirt and doll is attached to stand. Papers are pulled out and the fortunes are written in French. Courtesy Barbara Earnshaw-Cain.

Plate 90. 10½″ Marked F.G. Fortune Telling Doll. Glass eyes, closed mouth and all original. The papers that make up the skirt pull out to reveal a hand written "fortune" in French. Courtesy Kimport Dolls.

Fouquet and Douville

Plate 91. 26″ Made by Fouquet & Douville (1891-1893). Has flirty non-sleeping eyes that are operated with two strings through holes at back of head. Closed mouth and on French jointed wood and composition body. Marks: 103/16/X.

H

The maker of the French dolls marked with an "H" is not known. They were made about 1880 and are found on a combination of wood and composition jointed bodies. The quality can differ greatly with these dolls and the highest prices are paid for the perfect, beautiful examples only.

Plate 92-93. 21½" Marked: 3-H, incised on head. Large, beautiful blue paperweight eyes. May be original clothes. On Jumeau style jointed composition body. Courtesy Kimport Dolls.

H.G.

Henri and Grange Guimonneau and Cie (Company) were the makers of the very rare French dolls that are marked with an H.G. and Paris. Since they were only in business for a short time (1879 to 1885) their dolls are much harder to locate to add to a collection. The Guimonneau dolls came with kid or composition jointed bodies and they produced both closed and open mouth dolls. As with most French makers they made dolls dressed in luxury clothes and also with clothes of lesser materials and time to cut the cost of the doll.

Plate 94. 24½″ Incised: Paris H.G. 11. A very rare and lovely doll. Has open/closed mouth with shaded and accented lips. Ears are pierced, and she may be all original with mohair wig and original clothes. She is on French jointed body marked: Jumeau Medaille D'or Paris. Replaced shoes. Courtesy Frasher Auctions.

Plate 95. Close up of head of the French doll marked: Paris H.G. 11. Courtesy Frasher Auction.

Jullien

Jullien, Jeune (Junior) made Bébés, soldiers (Zouaves), Nankeen dolls and a general line of dolls. He made ordinary and deluxe dolls, had ladies, brides, peasants, Bébés with trousseaux, young girls, swimmers and bathers. His dolls had both swivel necks and molded one-piece shoulder date and heads, talking dolls and one that talked and walked in 1895. He made dolls with open and closed mouths as most of the French makers did.

Jullien was in business from 1863 to 1904. In 1904, his firm became a member of the Société Francaise de Fabrication de Bébé et Jouets (S.F.B.J.) In 1900, Jullien won a bronze medal at the Pairs Exposition.

Jullien dolls are marked with the name "Jullien" or with the initials "JJ." In 1892, Jullien advertised L'Universal, and the label can be found on some of his doll bodies.

Plate 96. 19″ Doll by Jullien. Marks: J 6 J. Closed mouth and on French jointed composition body. Feathered eyebrows, pierced ears and may have original wig. Courtesy Frasher Auctions.

Plate 97. 22″ Marked: Jullien 8. Open mouth, mohair wig over cork pate, pierced ears and early French jointed body with straight wrists. Courtesy Frasher Auctions.

Jumeau

Pierre Francois Jumeau started business in 1846 with a partner, M. Belton. It is known that by 1851 they were making dolls as at the London World Exposition their very lavish dressed dolls caused a great sensation due to the newest and most up-to-date tailoring. These early dolls had kid bodies which came in white, pale cream or pink and were made with gussets at the elbows, hips and knees, with stitching forming the fingers and toes. On the larger dolls the fingers and toes were stuffed separately.

Prior to 1862 Jumeau dolls had one piece shoulders and heads, and in 1862 Jumeau patented a swivel head, although it should be noted that Mademoiselle Calixte Huret had applied for a patent for a swivel head in 1861. All the Jumeau dolls of this period had closed mouths and all were called "poupee Parisienne." In the last part of the 1860's and the first years of the 1870's, Jumeau was making the same kind of dolls, but now he was producing his own doll head in a factory located at Montreuill Sous-Bois. It is important to note that at the 1873 Exhibition at Vienna it was said, "M. Jumeau of Paris, the first and most important doll making house, has freed us from our former obligation to have the foreigner (Germany) furnish us with porcelain doll heads. M. Jumeau has established at Montreuill, near Paris, a factory where he makes dolls heads of enameled porcelain with the greatest perfection. He has surpassed in beauty the products that we used to buy from Saxony." In reference to the above statement, enameled porcelain could mean the facial colors applied or a high gloss "china" style painting. It would also lead one to believe that both Belton and all "poupee Parisienne"— fashion doll heads — were made in Germany.

At his Vienna Exhibition, Jumeau won a gold medal as well as the Medal of Progress, and that same year the medal of cooperation went to four representatives of the Maison P.F. Jumeau: Emile Jumeau (youngest son of founder), Madame Blanche Pannier, Mademoiselle Elisa Cadet and Oscar Rinders.

It was during this part of the 1870's that the two sons of Pierre Jumeau, Georges, the elder who was to inherit the factory and Emile, the youngest, tried to persuade their father that it was time for change. Georges, with patience and ingenuity, obtained small reforms and was leading into major changes when he died. The loss of his eldest son crushed Pierre Jumeau, and he lost his desire to work and grew old rapidly. His second son, Emile, who wanted to be an architect, succeeded him.

After Emile Jumeau took over the operation of the business, he created Bebes or children and baby types. At this time period "unbreakable" bébés appeared in Paris. "Unbreakable" was referring to composition, jointed bodies. Until then the full name of Jumeau did not appear on the dolls, and the word Bébé was used for the first time. He (Emile) has been credited with the invention of the Bébé and rightly so. His dolls caused such a stir in France that there were rumors and reports (newspapers and competitors), and articles from papers such as "Figaro" which made statements like . . . "even though virulent circulars have been written about him, M. Jumeau is and remains the inventor of the Bébé which bears his name, and no one else has the right to any claim to it."

After Pierre Francois Jumeau took out the patent for a swivel head in 1862, no others are shown until his son Emile took out several. In 1882, Bru and Jumeau took out a patent on a mechanical boat. In 1885, Jumeau took out a patent for eyelids that dropped down over the eyes. In 1886, he got another patent to eliminate the space left when the eyelid was in an open position. Also that same year he received a patent for an unbreakable doll, and a patent for sleeping eyes with lashes.

Emile Jumeau registered the trademark "Bébé Jumeau" in 1886 (in U.S. in 1888) and the same year one for "Bébé Prodige" and in 1896 for "Bébé Francais."

As to medals, the following are listed: 1844 Paris (Belton & Jumeau) honorable mention for doll clothes. 1851 London-gold medal; 1885 Paris-silver; 1867 Paris-Silver; 1873 Vienna-gold; 1876 Philadelphia-gold; 1878 Paris-gold; 1879 Melbourne-gold; 1884 New Orleans-gold; 1885 Antwerp-Diploma de Honour; 1885 Paris-gold; and in 1886 named Chevalier de la Legion d'Honneur (Knight in the Legion of Honer).

In 1887, Buffalo Bill Cody visited Europe and purchased a Jumeau doll. This particular style face doll has become known as the "Cody" or "Long Face" Jumeau. Now they are also referred to as "Triste" Jumeaus. "Triste" in French means "sad, unhappy, mournful, etc" and since there is no exact exchange word for the American slang term of "long face" European collectors began calling this Jumeau model "Triste," which does to do justice to the dolls as they are not pouty, nor unhappy looking dolls at all. The modeling of the face, especially the cheeks are longer than regular Jumeau dolls, and therefore the American usage of the term "long face" means the size of features, not the "look on the doll's face."

During the 1890's Jumeau turned to quantity and advertisements said (1892), "The Maison Jumeau makes two new models with differences in price of 20 percent and 40 percent, but with the same irreproachable quality remaining and not carrying the Jumeau name."

In 1889, Jumeau joined the Sociéte Francaise de Fabrication de Bébé et Jouets. (S.F.B.J.) Sample marks: Incised: E.J., Tété Deposé/Jumeau and also the red stamp; Tété/Jumeau. Blue or red stamps and/or stickers on bodies: Bébé Jumeau/Diplomé d'Honneur or Jumeau/Medaille d'or/Paris and some: Deposé/Jumeau.

Plate 98. 20″ Marked: E. 9 J. and red check artist marks. Body is marked: Jumeau Medaille D'or Paris. Jointed body with straight wrists, closed mouth and pierced ears. Almond-shaped paperweight set eyes. The mark on the head is incised and the mark on the body is stamped. Courtesy Frasher Auctions.

Plate 99. 14″ Marked: E.J. on head and is on jointed Jumeau body with straight wrists. Closed mouth.

Plate 100. 15″ Socket head on jointed wood and composition body. Open/closed mouth, pierced ears and marked: E.6 J. on head. Body marked: Jumeau/Medaille D'or/Paris. All original clothes, parasol and pin, original wig but is missing hat.

Plate 101. 26″ "Bébé Phonographe" by Jumeau. Marks: DéposéTétéJumeau 11. Bisque head with open mouth, composition body stamped: Jumeau Medaille D'or Paris. Has removable metal chest plate and key wind and plunger to player records. The phonograph has trademark: Phonorape Systems Lioet Bte S.G.D.G. Patent Marque H L deFabrique and the wax cylinder is marked: Bébé Phonographe Bte S.G.D.G. Marque H L Depose Petite Papa 5. Courtesy Frasher Auctions.

Plate 102. 18″ Two-face Jumeau with one side smiling and other crying. Has voice box with pull strings to make it "cry." Unusual large size. Courtesy Kimport Dolls.

Plate 103. Shows the crying side of the two-face Jumeau. Courtesy Kimport Dolls.

Plate 104. 15″ Portrait Jumeau with head incised: 7, low on socket. Ball-jointed composition body with straight wrists and body has blue stamp: Jumeau Medaille D'or Paris. Set paperweight eyes, closed mouth and has original wig and cork pate. Dress is old commercially made and has Jumeau marked shoes. Courtesy Florence Maine.

Plate 105. Three tiny Jumeaus, all marked head and body. Left to right: #1 in a copy of a Bru dress, #2 is 11″ tall with brown eyes and another #2 that is a "portrait" Jumeau. Courtesy Marlowe Cooper.

Plate 106. 11″ Black Jumeau with color fired into bisque, rosey lips, black glass eyes, and pierced ears. Completely original clothes. Courtesy Marlowe Cooper.

Plate 107. 34″ "Long Face" Jumeau also called "Cody" Jumeau. On Jumeau marked body, closed mouth and large brown paperweight eyes. Shown in buggy is 20″ "Long Face" Jumeau with marked Jumeau body with straight wrists. Courtesy Turn of Century Antiques.

Plate 108. 26½" Flirty Eye Jumeau. Has lever in back of head to operate eyes, which can be moved from side to side and to open and close. Open mouth and in original shoes, old wig and hat. Head is marked Tete Jumeau Bte. S.G.D.G. and is on typical Jumeau body. Courtesy Barbara Earnshaw-Cain.

Plate 109. 30″ "Long Face-Cody" Jumeau. Head is unmarked and body: Jumeau/Medaille D'or. Outfit is made from old materials, and she has her original Jumeau marked shoes. Courtesy Jeanne Haskins.

Plate 110. 21″ Long Face Jumeau with applied ears and marked: 10, on head. Marked Jumeau body with straight wrists. May be original clothes. Courtesy Kimport Dolls.

Plate 111. 21″ Marked with stamp on head: Déposé/Tété Jumeau. On French fully-jointed composition body. Closed mouth, pierced ears and dressed in new outfit. Courtesy Kimport Dolls.

Plate 112. 27″ "Long Face" or "Cody" Jumeau marked only: 13, on head. Straight wrists, pierced ears and closed mouth. Courtesy Marlowe Cooper.

Plate 113. 29″ "Long Face" Jumeau also called "Cody Jumeau." Head marked with size number 14 and body marked: Jumeau/Medaille D'or. All original clothes and replaced wig. Courtesy Jay Minter.

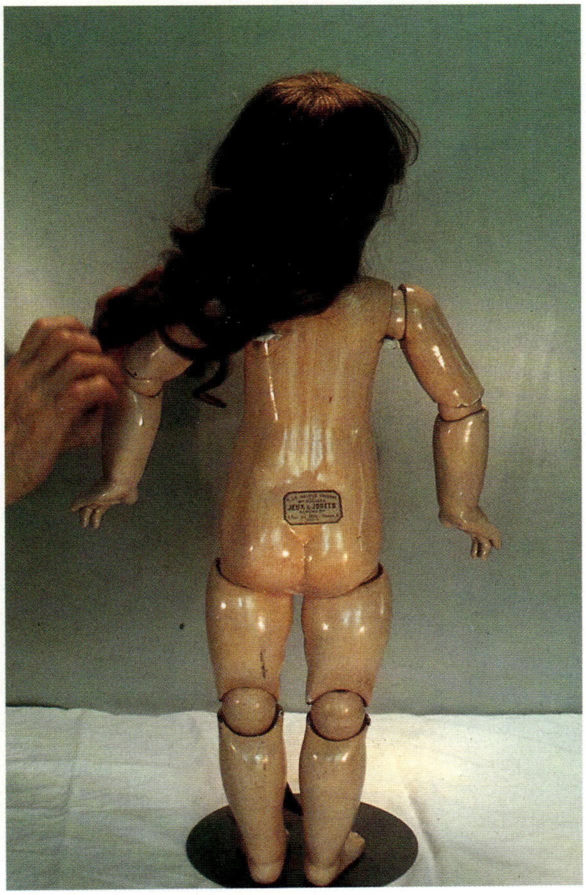

Plate 114. Correct body for the "Long Face" Jumeau. Courtesy Marlowe Cooper.

Plate 115. 11″ #2 Jumeau marked head and body. Brown glass eyes, closed mouth and pierced ears. Courtesy Marlowe Cooper.

Plate 116. 10½″ Tiny Jumeau marked head and body. Brown glass eyes, closed mouth and pierced ears. Courtesy Marlowe Cooper.

Plate 117. 10¼″ Marked head and body Jumeau. Blue glass eyes, closed mouth and pierced ears. Courtesy Marlowe Cooper.

Plate 118. 19″ Closed mouth Jumeau with pierced ears, pale bisque and socket head on jointed body with straight wrists. Marks: Depose Tete Jumeau/Bete S.G.D.G.-8/in red stamp on head. Blue stamp on body: Jumeau Medaille D'Or Paris. Courtesy Joanna Brunken.

Plate 120. 13″ Bisque socket head on composition body marked: DEPOSE/E 4 J/with a "vl" and "h" painted on. Both have closed mouths and paperweight eyes, with one having blue eyes and the other brown. Courtesy Reins Collection.

Plate 119. Typical Jumeau marked composition body with straight wrists. "Straight wrists" means the arms are unjointed at the wrists, although there may be a mold line where the jointing would have been. French knees are flush and plain where Germans enjoyed the details of dimples, rolls of fat and much knee detail.

Plate 121. 25½″ Incised: Jumeau, along with Jumeau stamp. On jointed marked Jumeau body. Old, maybe original clothes. Closed mouth, pierced ears. Courtesy Kimport Dolls.

Plate 122. 19″ Marked: Déposé/Tété Jumeau/Bte. S.G.D.G./sh on head and has: Jumeau/Medaille D'or/Paris stamped in blue on body. Open/closed mouth with white space between lips. The body is jointed composition.

Plate 123. 23″ Tête Jumeau #10 with brown glass eyes, closed mouth and marked Jumeau body. Copy of an original dress. Courtesy Marlowe Cooper.

Plate 124. 11″ Jumeau with 8″ head circumference. Closed mouth, brown paperweight eyes, pierced ears and cork pate. Courtesy Elizabeth Burke.

Plate 125. 34″ Jumeau with closed mouth and on composition jointed body. Applied, pierced ears. Marks: TêteJumeau/Bte. and on body: Jumeau Medaille D'or Paris S.G.D.G. Courtesy Turn of Century Antiques.

Plate 126. 34″ Marked: Tête Jumeau Bte on head and Jumeau Medaille D'or Paris S.G.D.G. Many of the Jumeau dolls have applied ears, especially the large ones. This shows an applied ear and one can see that the head and ear are made separately then process fired together. Courtesy Turn of Century Antiques.

Plate 127. 20″ Incised E.J. Large paperweight eyes, closed mouth and applied ears. On marked Jumeau body with straight wrists.

Plate 128. 20″ Marked on head, stamped in red: DEP/Tété Jumeau/8. Body is marked, in an oval: BébéJumeau/Diplome d Honneur. Blue eyes, hair lashes, pierced ears and open mouth. Courtesy Pat Timmons.

Plate 129. 20″ Closed mouth marked Téte Jumeau on head and body. Closed mouth and almond-shaped eyes. Jointed composition body.

Plate 130. 22″ Open mouth Jumeau with six molded teeth, pierced ears, and on jointed body with torso made in two sections and taped, has two holes on side for pull strings with cryer box in torso. Red stamp Tete Jumeau, on head and blue stamp Bebe Jumeau/S.G.D.G. Depose on body. (Sitting) 24″ open mouth Jumeau that is smiling. Jointed body with head marked: red stamp—slightly smudged/June Jumeau/10 D.E.P. Courtesy Joanna Brunken.

Plate 131. 25″ Open mouth Jumeau that is incised 1907 and has the red stamp: Tête Jumeau, over it. Pierced ears and on Jumeau jointed body. Courtesy Jay Minter.

Plate 132. 13″ Brown fired-in color Jumeau with the head marked, 1907. Has open mouth, black glass eyes and on Jumeau jointed composition body. Courtesy Kimport Dolls.

Plate 133. 22″ Open mouth marked: J and Tête Jumeau, blue stamp. On jointed composition French body. Courtesy Kimport Dolls.

Plate 134. 16″ On jointed composition/wood Schmitt body with straight wrists. Pink wash over eyes, closed mouth, pierced ears. "Portrait" Jumeau head with almond-shaped eyes.

Plate 135. 17″ All original Jumeau that has original box. Marks: Tete Jumeau/7. Open mouth and on jointed composition body. Made in 1890's.

Plate 136. 24½″ "Portrait Jumeau" marked with a 4 on head and is on marked Jumeau body with straight wrists. Pink wash over eyes, on chin and in ears. Closed mouth and pierced ears. Courtesy Cathy Turchan.

Plate 137. 7½″ 1939 Jumeau with sleep eyes, bisque head and on jointed composition and wood body. Open mouth and completely original. Paper label on skirt. Courtesy Jo Fasnacht.

Plate 138. 20″ Jumeau marked in red: Deposé Tété Jumeau Bte S.G.D.G., followed by artist's marks and 9. Old clothes that may be original as wig may be also. Courtesy Shirlie Glass.

Plate 139. 16″ marked: Deposé Tété Jumeau Bi S.G.D.G. with open mouth, jointed Jumeau body and pierced ears. Courtesy Shirlie Glass.

Plate 140. Very late 14″ tall Jumeau with painted bisque head, jointed body, all original with original tag and dating from the 1930's when Jumeau was part of the S.F.B.J. group. Courtesy Shirlie Glass.

Plate 141. 16″ Dressed in original provincial costume and has her original fur caracul wig. Closed mouth and marked Jumeau body has straight wrists. Courtesy Barbara Earnshaw-Cain.

Lejeune

Plate 142. 22″ beautifully modeled bisque head that is marked: which is the trademark of Louis-Aime Lejeune, located at 66 Avenue de Bois-Guimer, Saint Maur des Fosse and her registration number dates from Dec. 14, 1915. This head is modeled after Dorothy Ward, a then-famous stage actress.

Limoges

The A. Lanternier & Cie were the main makers of dolls located at Limoges, Frances and started business in 1855 making decorated porcelain pieces. It was much later when they began to make dolls' heads and most of these dolls will be marked with such names as "Lorraine," "Favorite," "La Georgienne," etc.

LIMOGES
A L

FABRICATION
FRANCAISE
AL & Cie
LIMOGES

Plate 143. 22½" "Toto" marked: Toto/Limoges. Character bisque head with open/closed mouth, set glass eyes. Molded tongue and two upper teeth. Courtesy Kimport Dolls.

Plate 144. 14″ marked: Petite Francaise/J France V/(anchor sign)Liane. Set eyes, open mouth with molded teeth and jointed body with straight wrists. Courtesy Elizabeth Burke.

Plate 145. 15″ with 9½″ head circumference. Blue paperweight eyes, open mouth with four porcelain teeth and marked on head: Depose/Fabrication/No. 3/Ed Tasson/Alec/Limoges/(figure with girl with wings)/La Georginne. Courtesy Elizabeth Burke.

Plate 146. 17½″ Marked: Masson/J C/Lorraine/N 20/Al. & Co./Limoge. Flapper style doll on adult, slim body of composition. Open/closed mouth with painted teeth. Courtesy Kimport Dolls.

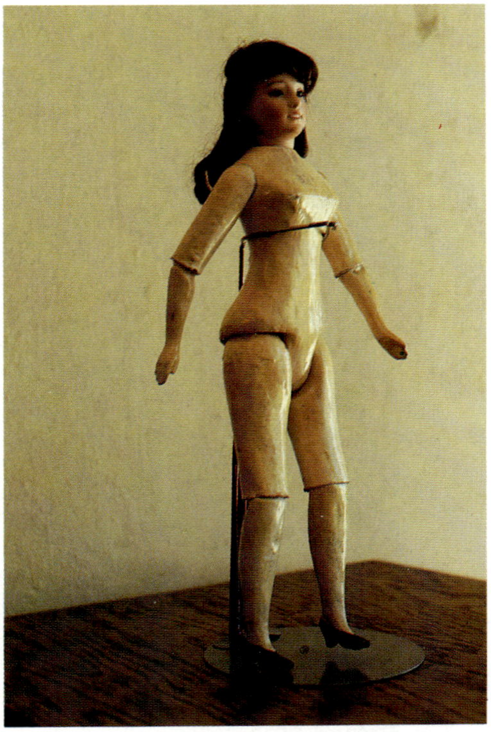

Plate 147. 18″ Lady doll on unusual body that has an adult figure and jointed at elbows and knees. The legs are strung into the hips, and she has molded-on heeled slippers. The bisque head is thin with closed mouth and painted teeth. The eyes are glass and set. Mark: J.E. Masson/Limoges, on head. Courtesy Turn Of Century Antiques.

Plate 148. 14″ with 8½″ head circumference and marked on head: Petite Francaise/France/J (anchor sign)/Liane. Set blue eyes, open mouth with molded teeth and on jointed composition body with straight wrists. Courtesy Elizabeth Burke.

Plate 149. 20″ Marked: Fabrication Francaise ALEC Limoges A8. Open mouth with molded teeth. Jumeau style jointed body with jointed wrists. Face also has a very Jumeau look. Courtesy Shirlie Glass.

Plate 150. 12″ marked: Limoges/France/J.B./3. Close up photo shows the set eyes, open mouth with teeth, unusual eyebrow treatment with high flying strokes. Lip painting is unusual also. Courtesy Elizabeth Burke.

Plate 151. 12″ with 7½″ head circumference. Set eyes, open mouth with teeth and marked: Limoges/France/J.B./3. Original human hair wig and has extremely long painted lashes. The eyebrows are one stroke with "fly-a-way" brush strokes above them. Courtesy Elizabeth Burke.

Mascotte

Mascotte dolls were made by Mays Freres and Cie from 1890 to 1897, and then this firm became a part of Jules Steiner from 1898 to the 1900's.

Plate 152. 16″ Bébé Mascotte made by May Freres Cie from 1890 to 1897. Closed mouth, paperweight eyes and on jointed composition French body. Courtesy Kimport Dolls.

Plate 153. 21″ Bébé Mascotte with a Jumeau look. Head is incised "J," has closed mouth and is on jointed French body. Made by May Freres Cie in the 1890's. Courtesy Jeanne Haskins.

Plate 154. Beautiful mechanical made by Vichy. Has music box that plays a lovely tune operated by pulling a cord. The dolls actually operated by winding a key. Mother gives bottle to baby and turns head. Wood carved hands. Both have closed mouths. Courtesy Shirlie Glass.

Plate 155. Close up of the beautiful face on the early mechanical that has adult-like modeling and is all original. Courtesy Shirlie Glass.

Plate 156. 10″ tall French mechanical. Bisque head with closed mouth, all original and doll is mounted on three wheel metal platform and when key is wound the doll turns its head, raises and lowers one hand. Key is marked: France. Courtesy Frasher Auctions.

Plate 157. 20″ Mechanical made by Jumeau. Stands on red velvet-covered base with music box. Holds powder puff in one hand and mirror in other. Both arms and head moves. Courtesy Barbara Earnshaw-Cain.

Plate 158. 20″ Marked Jumeau mechanical that stands on red velvet-covered music box. Holds bottle of perfume in one hand and hankie in other. Both arms and head move. Courtesy Barbara Earnshaw-Cain.

Plate 159. Mechanical nurse and cart with baby. Doll is marked: S.F.B.J. and is all original. The baby is all original and made of celluloid. Nurse walks and pulls the cart. There is a store sticker on bottom of the cart: Au Nain Bleu G. Fauvet, followed by address and Paris. Courtesy Barbara Earnshaw-Cain.

Plate 160. All original (except shoes) mechanical girl pulling cart. Both dolls have open mouths and heads are marked: S.F.B.J. 301. Sizes are 13″ and 10″. Courtesy Barbara Earnshaw-Cain.

Plate 161. 23″ All original marked Jumeau mechanical with open mouth, pewter hands with one holding cigarette holder which moves to the mouth. Courtesy Kimport Dolls.

Plate 162. Close up of the marked Jumeau smoking mechanical. Has open mouth with no teeth and ivory-tipped cigarette holder. Courtesy Kimport Dolls.

Plate 163. 16″ tall (20″ including music box) marked: Dep. Tété Jumeau on bisque head. Blue paperweight eyes, closed mouth, original fur wig, pierced ears and original clothing. Has five movements: pigs ears and tail move, mallet moves up and down, head turns several ways and plays a French tune. Courtesy Elizabeth Burke.

Plate 164. 18″ French mechanical with exquisite bisque head. Glass eyes and pale bisque. Adult modeled face, and she is all original. She is on wheels, is key wound and waltzes. Courtesy Barbara Earnshaw-Cain.

Plate 165. Kicking, crying Jules Steiner with open mouth and two rows of teeth. Head turns from side to side and arms move up and down as doll kicks. Key wound. Courtesy Frasher Doll Auctions.

Plate 166. 24″ incised B.M. for Bébé Mothereau. Made by Alexandre Celestin Tiburee who used this trademark. The firm was in business from 1880 to 1895. Closed mouth and applied ears. These dolls are as rare as the marked A.T.'s and H's. Courtesy Carol and Elliot Zirlin.

Pannier - Papier Mache

Plate 167. 12" All original doll made by Madame Pannier and marked: P. 4 in red high on head, and this part of mark is incised. H 7 is written in red low on neck. Has fully stamped Jumeau body. Closed mouth. Courtesy Lori Weston.

Plate 168. Close up of face of the P. 4 marked doll made by Madame Pannier and incised P. 4. Courtesy Lori Weston.

Plate 169. 16" Made of papier mache and is jointed at shoulders and hips as well as the neck. Has gold painted-on boots and an adult face. Original closed are that of a French maid. Closed mouth and glass eyes. Courtesy Jo Fasnacht.

Plate 170. 14" French papier mache of 1830s. Painted eyes, cloth body with wood carved hands. Original Turkish costume, painted hair and beard far under chin. Hair mustache. Courtesy Kimport Dolls.

Paris Bébé

Dolls marked with Paris Bébé were by Danel & Cie who were in business from 1889 to 1895. In 1889 they registered in France "Paris Bébé" with the drawing of the Eiffel Tower, and in 1891 they registered "Bébé Francais." Jumeau registered "Bébé Francais" in 1896, so may have had control of this firm by then.

The bisque heads will be marked: Paris Bébé/Tête Depose or Tête Depose/Paris Bébé. The jointed bodies will be marked (stamp or sticker) with the Eiffel Tower/Paris Bébé/Brevete.

Plate 171. 22″ Marked: Tête Depose Paris Bébé 9 and the jointed composition body is also marked: Paris Bébé. Closed mouth. Courtesy Frasher Auctions.

Plate 172. 11″ Marked: Paris Bébé. Is on French fully-jointed composition body and has open/closed mouth and glass paperweight eyes. Clothes may be original but trim has been added.

Plate 173. 21½″ Paris Bebe marked Tété Dep/9. Composition jointed French body, closed mouth and pierced ears. Made by Danel & Cie. Courtesy Jeanne Haskins.

Plate 174. 21½" Paris Bebe/9 with composition French jointed body, closed mouth and pierced ears. Made by Danel & Cie. Courtesy Jeanne Haskins.

Phenix

The Phenix marked dolls were designed by Henri Alexandre and were registered and patented by him in 1889 in Paris. In 1890 Alexandre advertised 30 different models of the doll. In 1892, he sold out to Tourrel who used the same advertisements. It was in 1895 that the Phenix trademark was registered by Mme. Marie Lafosse who was associated with the Jules Steiner firm. In 1900 the Jules Steiner company merged with the Jules Mettais firm. The mark with the Phenix, ★ is followed by a number which usually is 95, 94 or 92.

Plate 175. 21″ Phenix marked with five point star-93. Open/closed mouth, pierced ears and heavy painted brows. Old wig and clothes. French jointed body.

Plate 176. 22″ Phenix Bébé marked: ★ 90. Made by Henri Alexandre. Closed mouth and jointed French body with straight wrists. Courtesy Jeanne Haskins.

Plate 177. 21″ Stamped in red ink: Phenix and with ★ 93 incised. Closed mouth, jointed body with straight wrists. May be original dress and shoes. Courtesy Shirlie Glass.

R.D.

In 1856, Jean Delphieu took out a French patent for using pink cloth instead of kid on doll bodies. It must be noted that kid-bodied R.D. dolls are very rare. The majority of R.D. marked dolls will be on French jointed bodies. Rabery-Delphieu won a silver medal at Amsterdam in 1883 and a silver medal in Paris in 1889.

The dolls will be marked with "R.D." on the back of the head and some with "Bébé Rabery" and a few with "Bébé de Paris."

Plate 178. 15″ Marked on head: R. 2/0 D. and on body R. 4.D. Closed mouth and on French jointed body.

Plate 179. 26″ Marked: R.D. with closed mouth and on fully jointed body. Pierced ears and large paperweight eyes. Courtesy Jay Minter.

Plate 180. 19½″ Marked: R. 1 D. and she has a wide open mouth with rows of teeth on bottom and top. On French jointed composition body. Courtesy Josephine Wingfield.

Plate 181. 17" Rabery & Delphieu that dates from 1881. Wooden arms and legs with papier mache body. She has papier mache feet that are molded onto the wooden lower legs. Pierced ears and closed mouth. Marks: R.O.D.

Plate 182. 16″ Marked: R. 1 D. Has a closed mouth and is on a fully jointed French body. Courtesy Barbara Earnshaw-Cain.

Plate 183. 15″ Marked: R. 2-0 D. and made by Rabery & Delphieu. Closed mouth with jointed French body. Courtesy Jeanne Haskins.

Schmitt & Fils

Although Schmitt & Fils seems to have been around since 1863, it was not until 1867 they were listed as a toy maker. In 1877, they perfected a method of painting porcelain shoulder heads and took out a patent. They also patented all bisque Bébés in 1879. In 1883, they had taken out a patent for a layer of wax to be applied over bisque doll heads after the heads had been removed from the kilns. They obtained several patents for eye movements, including one in 1885 (in Germany) for controlling eye movement by a knob at the back of the head.

Schmitt & Fils composition bodies generally have complete free-motion balls at the shoulders and hips and a very flat bottom of the rear torso and the front crotch area drops very low between the legs. The Schmitt mark is generally stamped on the flat bottom. On kid bodies the mark is generally located between the rear joints of the hips.

Schmitt won a silver medal at Paris in 1878. From 1879 to 1890 they made the "Bébé Schmitt," and they discontinued business in 1891. Sample mark:

Plate 184. 11″ Schmitt & Fils marked: "Sch" in shield on both head and body. Closed mouth and jointed body with straight wrists. Courtesy Frasher Auctions.

Plate 185. Close up of face of the closed-mouth Schmitt & Fils marked with: "Sch," in shield on both head and body. A rare little doll. Courtesy Frasher Auctions.

Plate 186. 23″ Marked: SCH. Closed mouth and large paperweight eyes. Original wig. Courtesy Barbara Earnshaw-Cain.

Plate 187. 16″ Schmitt & Fils marked head and body. Jointed French body with straight wrists, closed mouth and may be original clothes. Courtesy Barbara Earnshaw-Cain.

Plate 188. 22½″ Schmitt & Fils with Schmitt body with large "free form" balls at joints. Very flat on seat area of body. Closed mouth and straight wrists. Marks: SCH. Courtesy Burnice Wallen.

Plate 189. 24″ Marked Schmitt with crossed hammers in a shield on head and body. Ball-jointed composition body with straight wrists. Closed mouth. Courtesy Kimport Dolls.

S.F.B.J.

The initials S.F.B.J. stand for Société Francaise de Fabrication de Bébés et Jouets. (Society for the manufacturing of dolls and toys). This society was formed in 1899 and known members were Bru, Jumeau, Fleishmann & Blodel, Rabery & Delphieu, Pintal & Godchaux, P.H. Schmitz, A. Bouchet, Jullien and Danel & Cie.

The reason the society was formed was to try and survive as French doll makers due to the overwhelming increase of German dolls sold and to adjust the costs to try and be competitive.

The most common mold numbers found are 60 and 301, although they can be very different in appearances. There are some composition and celluloid S.F.B.J. dolls, but the majority have bisque heads on composition bodies. Most of the bisque heads continued to be made at factories in the Montreuil area, and by 1911 S.F.B.J. advertised they were making 5,000,000 dolls a year at their Vincennes factory and by 1925 they had eight factories in production of dolls. In 1922, they advertised they made 7,000,000 dolls.

In 1911, they registered in France the trademarks: "Bébé Prodige," Bébé Jumeau," and Bébé Francaise in 1913, Bébé Triomphe" in 1920, "Bébé Parisana," "Bébé Moderne," "Le Seduisant" and "BébéParfait" in 1921.

In 1922, S.F.B.J. had 2,800 employees, and they claimed they were using 2,000 models which included many character and colored dolls, also walking, talking and kiss-throwing dolls. S.F.B.J. continued in business until the 1950's.

The director of S.F.B.J. was Fleischmann, and at the beginning of World War I he was deported, and his properties taken from him because he was an alien (German).

They are a vast amount of "dolly" faced dolls, but also some are extremely rare and are character molds. Most of the character molds are in the 200 series. Sample marks:

S F
B J

S.F.B.J.
239
PARIS

FABRICATION FRANCIASE
SFBJ
PARIS

Plate 190. 19" Marked: Depose/S.F.B.J./6, on back of head. Has composition and papier mache body with straight legs and is a walker. The head turns from side to side as the legs move. Courtesy Pauline Hoch.

Plate 191. 18″ S.F.B.J. body with open/closed smiling mouth, solid dome with painted hair and dimples. On fully jointed body and head marked: S.F.B.J./226/Paris/6. 28″ Marked: 12 S H 1030/DEP. Socket head on bisque shoulder plate and kid body with bisque lower arms. Metal mechanism to pull string from hole in back of head to open and close eyelids. Courtesy Joanna Brunken.

Plate 192. 20″ Bisque head with high coloring, sleep eyes with hair lashes, open mouth and earrings sewn onto bonnet. Jointed composition body and all original. Marks: Paris/France, in an oval with a 71 and 149, along with a 301 and an "R," in a circle beneath that. Under the mark is also a "B." Made after the French makers formed the Société Francaise de Fabrication de Bébé & Jouets. (S.F.B.J.) Courtesy Pat Timmons.

Plate 193. 29″ and marked: S.F.B.J. Paris. Set eyes with real hair lashes, open mouth with six teeth and is on fully jointed body and pierced ears. Courtesy Irene Brown.

Plate 194. 24″ Marked: S.F.B.J. 247 Paris. Bisque head with open mouth and teeth. Has open/closed mouth with upper teeth. Has fully jointed toddler body. Courtesy Barbara Earnshaw-Cain.

Plate 195. 17½″ Marked: S.F.B.J./60/Paris 1½. Has open mouth, sleep eyes and is on a crude papier mache and composition jointed body. Courtesy Kitty Best.

Plate 196. Left to right: 16½″ solid dome socket head with painted hair, open mouth and set jewel eyes. Marks: SFBJ/227/Paris. Next is a 16″ with unhappy expression, set jewel eyes, painted hair and an open/closed mouth with six molded teeth above and two below. Marks: SFBJ/233/Paris. 14½″ with painted hair, set jewel eyes, open/closed mouth and marked: SFBJ/226/Paris. All have jointed composition bodies with center only having the SFBJ paper label on body. Courtesy Reins Collection.

Plate 197. 15½″ marked: S.F.B.J. 229. Has laughing open mouth, set "jewel" glass eyes and has voice box in jointed composition body. Courtesy Kimport Dolls.

Plate 199. 19½″ Marked S.F.B.J. 252 pouty with glass eyes, closed pouty mouth and on five-piece toddler body. Courtesy Kimport Dolls.

Plate 198. 15″ Marked: S.F.B.J. 251 with open mouth and molded tongue and two upper teeth. Set eyes and on five bent-limb baby body of composition. Courtesy Kimport Dolls.

Plate 200. 14½″ Socket head on fully-jointed French body. Open/closed mouth with two modeled upper teeth, flocked hair and blue "jewel" glass eyes. Marks: S.F.B.J. 235. Courtesy O.D. Gregg.

Plate 201. 17″ Socket head on fully-jointed French body with open mouth, set eyes with lashes and painted lashes below eyes only. Marks: S.F.B.J. 301/Paris/6. Courtesy Kathy Walters.

Plate 202. 24″ Incised on head: S.F.B.J. 230/Paris 10. The composition and wood jointed body is marked Jumeau Paperweight eyes and open mouth. Courtesy Frasher Auctions.

Plate 203. 14″ Harlequin marked: S.F.B.J. 301/Paris. Open mouth, white bisque with painted design, no wig and all original clothes. Composition jointed body, sleep eyes with hair lashes. Courtesy Kimport Dolls.

Plate 204. 10″ tall with 6½″ head circumference with girl marked: S.F.B.J. 301, pupiless black eyes/lashes, open mouth with upper teeth. The boy is marked: S.F.B.J. 251 with glass eyes, open mouth with molded tongue and two upper teeth. Courtesy Elizabeth Burke.

Plate 205. 14″ Stamped S.F.B.J. papier mache doll all original in regional clothes. Referred to as a "Baptime Doll" and reportedly given to children at their Baptisms. Doll opens at waist and holds candy or small toys. Courtesy Shirlie Glass.

Plate 206. Left to right: 16″ S.F.B.J. 233 "Screamer" and shown in other photo. 18″ marked: 2X on the head with bisque socket head, open mouth and on French jointed body, but maker unknown. 22″ Jumeau Portrait fashion, all kid body and bisque head on bisque shoulder plate. Courtesy Marion & Elsie Reins.

Plate 207. 14″ Marked: S.F.B.J./60/Paris/2/0. Set eyes, open mouth with four teeth and on 10-piece jointed body and has original costume. The stomach of this doll is padded with straw and wrapped in cheese cloth to give the effect of a heavier man's stomach. Courtesy Penny Pendlebury.

Plate 208. 20″ Incised S.F.B.J. 7, dressed in original clothes and shoes (hat may be added). She is a walker and cries as she walks. Open mouth and straight wrists. Courtesy Shirlie Glass.

Plate 209. French Wedding Party. Left to right 18″ Marked: F.G., in scroll on jointed composition body. 21″ Marked: SFBJ/247/Paris/6. With open/closed mouth, stuck out tongue and two upper teeth. On jointed toddler body. 19″ Pale bisque socket head with closed mouth and white area between lips, caracul wig and on jointed "Schmitt style" body, maker unknown. 18″ Bride with head marked: S.F.B.J./238/Paris/4 and has S.F.B.J. stamp on back of torso. Open mouth with four teeth and on wood and composition jointed adult body. 18″ marked: S.F.B.J. 236/Paris/8 with open/closed mouth and two upper teeth. Jointed toddler body. 19″ Marked: Steiner/Paris/Fre A 12 and Le Petit Parisien/Bébé Steiner, on body. Jointed composition body with straight wrists. Courtesy Marion and Elsie Reins.

Plate 210. Left to right: 14½″ marked: S.F.B.J. label on body, open mouth with five teeth and on typical French jointed body. 14½″ Marked: S.F.B.J./226/Paris on head and "#2" on feet. Solid dome bisque head with painted hair and has open/closed mouth. 15″ marked: 227 on head with solid dome. Open/closed mouth and on jointed body. Courtesy Marion & Elsie Reins.

Steiner, Jules

Jules Nichols Steiner operated the "Société Steiner" from 1852 to 1892 when the successor to the firm was Amedee LaFosse. A short time later the Widow LaFosse is listed as owner (1892-1899). It was in 1895 that Henri Alexandre (Maker of Bébé Phenix) and May Freres Cie (maker of Bébé Mascotte) mergered with the Steiner company. In 1899, Jules Mettais took over operating the company, and in 1906 Edmond Daspres was the successor.

Steiner won a silver medal at Paris in 1878, a gold medal at Paris in 1889, received the Diplome d'Honneur in 1890 and in 1891 received "Hors Concours" award. Almost all the awards were made during the time Jules Steiner was head of the firm.

The "wire eye" Steiner was based on the 1880 patent. Many Jules Steiner dolls have a glass pupil and iris that are set into an opaque white eyeball and will be marked with the name Steiner. Also a separate big toe is a Steiner characteristic. They seldom have cork pates but ones made of cardboard (pressed) that are generally colored with a purple wash.

It was in 1889 that this firm registered a girl with a banner and the words "le Petit Parisien" or "Medaille d'or/Pairs/1889. They introduced "Bébé Premier Pas" (walking doll) and "Bébé Marcheur (walking doll) in 1890.

By 1892 Amedee LaFosse was head of the firm and registered the trademark "Le Parisien." He seems to have died shortly after taking over and his widow ran the business until 1899 when Jules Mettais took over. It was 1899 when Jules Mettais registered "Phenix Bébé", "Bébé Liege" and "Bébé Merveilleuse". Mettails (Steiner) won a silver medal at the 1900 Paris Exposition and in 1901 registered "Bébé Modele" as a trademark and used the tradename "Mascotte." By 1906 Edmond Daspres was head of the Steiner firm, and he advertised "La Patricienne" in 1908.

The Jules Steiner company had many mechanical dolls, and Steiner heads are found on Motchmann & Huffner made bodies (bisque chest, upper arms, hips and lower legs) and it is not known if Steiner had the bodies made for them or if Motchmann & Huffner had the heads made for their bodies.

Sample marks:

J. Steiner
Bte S.G.D.G.
Fire A 12
Paris

Bourgoin

Ste C3
J. Steiner
B. S.G.D.G.

Plate 211. 19″ Marks: J Steiner Bte S.G.D.G. Paris Fire A 13. She has wire controlled sleep eyes and the eyes are incised with the Steiner patent. Closed mouth and is on a French Steiner jointed body with straight wrists. Courtesy Frasher Auctions.

Plate 212. 14″ Jules Steiner marked: Paris/A7.8. Body stamped: Bébé "Le Parisien"/Medaille d'or/Paris. papier mache and wood jointed body. Closed mouth and pierced ears.

Plate 213. 25″ Wire eye Steiner. Closed mouth, flat glass eyes, jointed composition body with straight wrists. Marks: J. Steiner/Bte S.G.D.G./Paris/Fre. A 17.

Plate 214. All the clothes, but the shoes are original on the wire Steiner, as is the wig. Most likely had a bonnet or hat to match.

Plate 215. Shows the side view of the original outfit on the wire-eyed Steiner, which has a pocket in the side seam that holds a lace-trimmed hankie.

Plate 216. Back view of the original clothes on the wire-eyed Steiner. Has tassels and beads hanging down from bow in back.

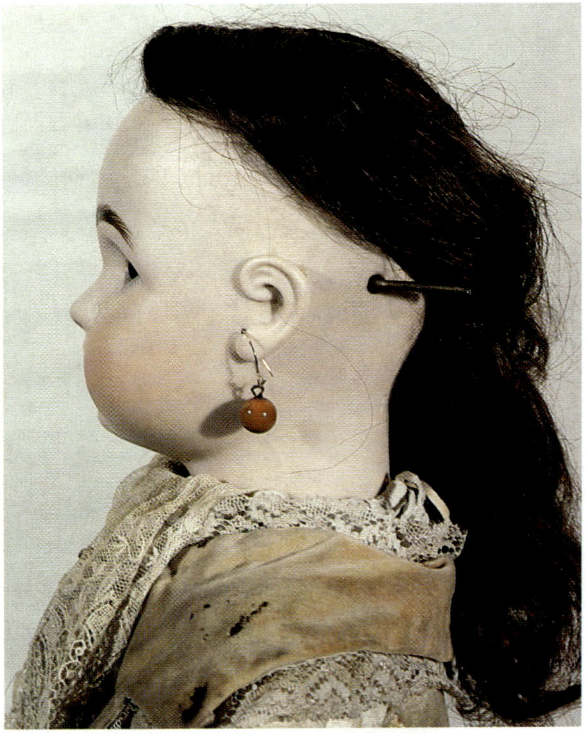

Plate 217. Shows the heavy wire mechanism that operates the eyes on the wire-eyed Steiner. Makes eyes open and close.

Plate 218. 23″ Incised: J Steiner/fre 15A. Steiner jointed body with rare pewter hands. Closed mouth, pierced ears and has paperweight glass eyes. Old clothes and shoes. Courtesy Marlowe Cooper.

Plate 219. 19″ Jules Steiner marked: Steiner/Paris/Fall and body is marked: Medaille D'or/Paris. Closed mouth and on fully jointed body. Courtesy Jay Minter.

Plate 220. 11″ Bébé J. Steiner le Petit Parisien." Socket head on Steiner jointed body with paper sticker with doll holding flag and: Medaille D'or/Paris/1889. Marks on head: J. Steiner/BTE S.G.D.G./Paris/Fi re/A3. In original box with original wardrobe. Courtesy Jay Minter.

Plate 221. 10″ Closed mouth tiny Jules Steiner that is marked: J Steiner/B15 SGDG/Paris/Fre A3. The body is marked with paper label that shows doll with flag and year 1889. All original and has her original box. This doll never had a wig. Courtesy Jo Fasnacht.

Plate 222. 18″ tall Jules Steiner marked: Steiner Paris Fre C 11. Has closed mouth and on Steiner jointed composition body with straight wrists. Courtesy Shirlie Glass.

Plate 223. 23″ Bourgoin Jules Steiner marked: J. Steiner Bte S.G.D.G. Sie C 3 J. Bourgoin St. Has closed mouth and all original clothes. Original wig restyled.

Plate 224. 17″ Steiner with closed mouth, set eyes, pierced ears and on fully marked Steiner body that is fully jointed. Marks: Fire A/Steiner Paris. Courtesy Barbara Earnshaw-Cain.

Plate 225. 23″ with 12½″ head circumference, pierced ears, blue paperweight eyes, closed mouth and has purple cardboard pate. Straight wrists with fingers nearly all same length. Pale bisque and head marked: J. Steiner/B te S.G.D.G./Paris/Fi re A 15. Body is marked: Medaille D'Or/Paris/1889. Courtesy Elizabeth Burke.

Plate 226. 20″ Key wound, kicking and crying Steiner with open mouth and two rows of teeth. Body parts are kid and composition. Courtesy Helen Draves.

Plate 227. "The Photograph." Left to right: 18″ Belton type with concave top to head with three holes. Closed mouth and ears are pierced into head. Jointed French body with straight wrists. 18″ Marked: Bru Jne/6. Closed mouth and rare all wood body with metal hands. 19″ Series Steiner that is marked both on head and body. Courtesy Marion and Elsie Reins.

Plate 228. 21″ Socket head on a Schmitt marked French body with straight wrists. Blue outlined eyes, full closed mouth, unpierced ears, cork pate and very "square" ridge to nose. Bisque is almost white with light pink wash over the eyes. Unmarked.

Plate 229. 19″ French doll that is only marked: 136. Her face resembles that of a "long face" Jumeau. Closed mouth, pierced ears, original mohair wig and wears factory original ivory color cotton dress with pink accents. Has jointed composition French body. Courtesy Frasher Auctions.

Plate 230. 13½″ Closed-mouth unmarked French child with one-piece bisque head and shoulder plate. Paperweight eyes, pierced ears and on kid body with bisque lower arms. Courtesy Kimport Dolls.

Plate 231. 17″ Unknown French bisque marked: Paris 5. Closed mouth, pierced ears and may be wearing original clothes and wig. French jointed body with straight wrists. Courtesy Frasher Auction.

Plate 232. 19½″ French "Poubout-type" with eyes with no pupils, open/closed mouth and on French jointed body. Courtesy Kimport Dolls.

Plate 233. 15″ Marked: Dep./44-26. French ball jointed body with straight wrists, paperweight set eyes, open mouth with four teeth. Courtesy Pat Timmons.

Plate 234. 21″ Marked: L C/DEP./P 11 G. Bisque socket head with open mouth and upper porcelain teeth. On fully jointed composition French body. Courtesy Kimport Dolls.

Plate 235. 14″ Marked: 204. Bisque head with closed mouth and paperweight eyes. Socket head on bisque shoulder plate. Kid body with bisque lower arms. May be German. Courtesy Kimport Dolls.

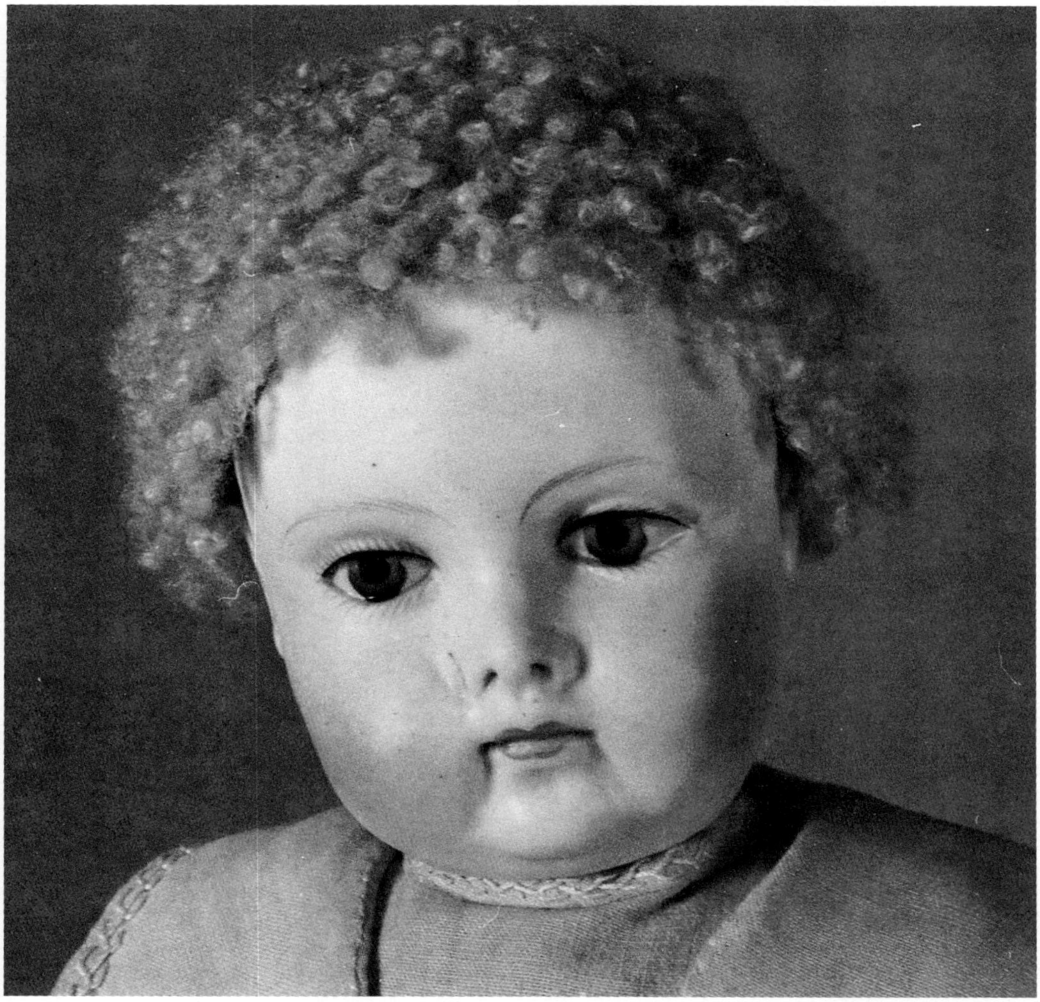

Plate 236-237. 15″-16″ Rohmer style child with white bisque and brown painted eyes. Closed mouth and round face. Caracul wig and on jointed French body with straight wrists. Courtesy Barbara Earnshaw-Cain.

Unis

Unis stands for Union Nationale Inter-Syndicali and was a kind of trade association, a type of "seal of approval" for trade goods, from consumers from manufacturers. Often the guide rules of this group of business, who were supposed to watch the quality of French export goods, were overlooked and some rather poor quality dolls escaped them, but there are some very nice Unis marked dolls also.

Unis started right after World War I and is still in effect today. Two doll companies are members: Poupee Bella and Petit Colin. There are other types of manufacturers in this group and they include makers of toys, sewing machines, tile, etc. Sample doll marks:

71 (Unis France) 149
301

Plate 238. Marked: Unis France on fully jointed French composition body. Open mouth, sleep eyes with lashes. Courtesy Frashers Doll Auctions.

Plate 239. 11½" Black French girl marked: Unis France, in oval. Open mouth and on five piece papier mache body. Glass black eyes and may be in original nurse outfit. Courtesy Kimport Dolls.

Price Guide

All Bisque Dolls

The following are prices for identified all bisque dolls that are French. The doll should be originally dressed, or re-dressed in old materials, have no chips, breaks or cracks, especially around the joints.

Swivel head with molded shoes: 4½″ - $650.00, 6″ - $800.00
Bare feet with swivel head: 5½″ - $700.00
Jointed elbows: 5½″ - $1,600.00
Jointed elbows and knees: 5½″ - $2,200.00
S.F.B.J. Unis, or other later French: 5″ - $350.00, 7″ - $450.00

Plate 1 .... $275.00
Plate 2 .... $800.00-1,200.00

A.T.

Prices listed are for dolls with correct body, beauty of bisque and originally or re-dressed in old materials that correctly suit the doll. There can be no damage such as a hairline crack, chip or any defects or the price will be less than half of the listed price. The following are sample marks:

A. 8 T.   AT N°3

Closed mouth: 14″ - $16,000.00, 18″ - $24,000.00, 24″ - $29,000.00, 26″ - $32,000.00
Open mouth (two rows of teeth): 14″ - $8,000.00, 18″ - $12,000.00, 24″ - $16,000.00

Plate 3 .... $17,000.00
Plate 4 .... $16,000.00

Belton-Types

Prices are for perfect dolls with no hairline cracks, chips and on correct bodies with straight wrists.

Child: 10″ - $995.00, 12″ - $1,150.00, 15″ - $1,600.00, 18″ - $1,900.00, 20″ - $2,200.00, 23″ - $2,500.00, 26″ - $3,000.00

Plate 5 .... $2,200.00
Plate 6 .... $2,300.00
Plate 7 .... $1,200.00
Plate 8 .... $1,500.00
Plate 9 .... $1,150.00
Plate 10 .... $1,150.00
Plate 11 .... $2,200.00
Plate 12 .... $1,150.00
Plate 13 .... $1,600.00

B.F.

Prices are for perfect bisque heads with no hairlines, chips or cracks and on nice body, closed mouth and nicely dressed:

Child: 12″ - $2,300.00, 17″ - $3,100.00, 20″ - $3,700.00, 24″ - $4,300.00, 27″ - $4,800.00

Plate 14 .... $2,700.00
Plate 15 .... $3,700.00

Bru

Bébé Brevete: 14″ - $8,000.00, 17″ - $10,000.00, 20″ - $14,000.00, 24″ - $17,500.00
Circle Dot Bébé: 16″ - $10,000.00, 19″ - $14,500.00, 23″ - $18,000.00
Black or Oriental: 16″ - $12,000.00+, 19″ - $16,000.00+
Bébé Teteur-Nursing Bru:
Early, excellent quality: 12″ - $4,400.00, 15″ - $6,500.00, 18″ - $8,200.00
Not as good quality, but still well done: 12″ - $2,100.00, 15″ - $3,700.00, 18″ - $4,700.00
Late with high bisque color of S.F.B.J. type: 12″ - $1,200.00, 15″ - $2,200.00, 18″ - $2,800.00
Bru Jne Bébé: 12″ - $6,200.00, 14″ - $7,400.00, 16″ - $9,000.00, 20″ - $12,000.00, 25″ - $18,000.00
Bru Jne R Bébé: 14″ - $4,500.00, 17″ - $4,900.00, 22″ - $6,300.00, 25″ - $7,300.00, 28″ - $8,000.00

Plate 16 .... $16,000.00
Plate 17 .... close-up
Plate 18 .... $15,000.00
Plate 19 .... side-view
Plate 20 .... $14,000.00
Plate 21 .... $16,000.00
Plate 22 .... close-up
Plate 23 .... $8,600.00
Plate 24 .... $9,300.00
Plate 25 .... $11,000.00
Plate 26 .... $9,300.00
Plate 27 .... $9,200.00
Plate 28 .... $6,000.00
Plate 29 .... $6,200.00
Plate 30 .... $15,500.00
Plate 31 .... $10,000.00
Plate 32 .... $18,000.00
Plate 33 .... $7,200.00
Plate 34 .... close-up

Court Doll

Plate 35 .... $6,000.00 up
Plate 36 .... side view
Plate 37 .... back view

DEP.

Closed mouth: 14″ - $1,200.00, 18″ - $1,800.00, 25″ - $2,600.00, 30″ - $3,000.00
Open Mouth: 14″ - $700.00, 18″ - $925.00, 25″ - $1,500.00, 30″ - $1,900.00

Walking, kissing, open mouth: 14″ - $950.00, 18″ - $1,200.00, 22″ - $1,500.00, 26″ - $1,800.00

Plate 38 . . . . $2,850.00
Plate 39 . . . . $1,500.00
Plate 40 . . . . $2,900.00

E.D.

Marked E.D. Bébé with excellent quality bisque, closed mouth, undamaged with no hairlines, chips and nicely dressed: 14″ - $2,100.00, 18″ - $2,500.00, 22″ - $2,900.00, 25″ - $3,500.00, 29″ - $4,000.00
Marked E.D. Bébé of lesser quality with bright red lips, rough bisque and rather crude papier mache body. Closed mouth: 14″ - $950.00, 18″ - $1,400.00, 22″ - $1,550.00
Marked E.D. Bébé with open mouth and excellent quality: 14″ - $1,400.00, 18″ - $1,900.00, 22″ - $2,400.00, 25″ - $2,800.00, 29″ - $3,200.00
Marked E.D. Bébé with open mouth of lesser quality: 14″ - $650.00, 18″ - $900.00, 22″ - $1,100.00

Plate 41 . . . . $2,200.00
Plate 42 . . . . $2,900.00
Plate 43 . . . . $2,100.00

Eden Bébé

Eden Bébé with closed mouth, excellent quality bisque and no damage: 15″ - $1,800.00, 18″ - $2,300.00, 22″ - $2,700.00, 26″ - $3,200.00
Eden Bébé with closed mouth, high color to bisque and dark red painted lips: 15″ - $650.00, 18″ - $1,000.00, 22″ - $1,300.00, 26″ - $1,600.00
Eden Bébé with open mouth and excellent bisque and no damage: 15″ - $1,000.00, 18″ - $1,500.00, 22″ - $2,000.00, 26″ - $2,500.00
Eden Bébé with open mouth, poor quality bisque and high color: 15″ - $450.00, 18″ - $700.00, 22″ - $950.00, 26″ - $1,100.00
Eden Bébé with ball jointed body and walking mechanism: 18″ - $825.00+, 24″ - $1,200.00

Plate 44 . . . . $2,600.00
Plate 45 . . . . $1,800.00
Plate 46 . . . . $1,900.00

Fashions

Prices are for dolls in perfect condition with no cracks, chips, nor repairs and in beautiful old or newer appropriate clothes.
Marked F.G. with swivel neck, all kid body: 14″ - $1,400.00, 17″ - $1,800.00
Marked F.G. with all kid body and one piece shoulder plate and head: 14″ - $700.00, 17″ - $1,600.00
Marked Jumeau body/number on head: 14″ - $2,100.00, 18″ - $3,400.00, 24″ - $4,800.00
Marked Huret or Rohmer: 16″ - $5,000.00, 20″ - $6,400.00 up
Huret Portrait Lady: 18″ - $9,800.00+
Articulated wood or blown kid bodies and limbs (some with bisque lower arms): 16″ - $3,000.00+, 20″ - $3,700.00+
Articulated with bisque lower legs and bisque, finely detailed lower legs and feet: 16″ - $3,600.00+, 20″ - $4,300.00+

Plate 47 . . . . $3,500.00+
Plate 48 . . . . $3,000.00+
Plate 49 . . . . $4,200.00
Plate 50 . . . . $5,000.00
Plate 51 . . . . $7,000.00
Plate 55 . . . . $5,000.00
Plate 56 . . . . $3,400.00
Plate 57 . . . . $5,200.00
Plate 58 . . . . $3,600.00
Plate 59 . . . . $1,100.00
Plate 60 . . . . $2,600.00
Plate 61 . . . . $2,100.00+
Plate 62 . . . . $3,200.00+
Plate 63 . . . . $1,800.00
Plate 64 . . . . $4,400.00
Plate 65 . . . . $4,200.00+
Plate 66-67 . . . . $5,000.00+
Plate 68 . . . . $3,200.00
Plate 69 . . . . $1,900.00
Plate 70 . . . . $3,200.00+
Plate 71 . . . . $1,500.00+
Plate 72 . . . . $2,600.00
Plate 73 . . . . close-up

F.G.

Child with closed mouth: excellent bisque, no damage and nicely dressed: 14″ - $2,600.00, 16″ - $2,800.00, 19″ - $3,200.00, 22″ - $3,500.00, 25″ - $4,200.00
Child with closed mouth, but high face color, no damage and well dressed: 14″ - $1,600.00, 16″ - $1,800.00, 19″ - $2,100.00, 22″ - $2,400.00
Child with open mouth, excellent quality bisque, no damage and nicely dressed: 14″ - $1,300.00, 16″ - $1,500.00, 19″ - $1,700.00, 22″ - $2,000.00
Child with open mouth, with high face color, no damage and well dressed: 14″ - $600.00, 16″ - $700.00, 19″ - $900.00, 22″ - $1,000.00
Marked F.G. Fashion: See Fashion Section.
Child on marked Gesland Body, bisque head on stocknet over wire frame body with bisque or composition lower limbs. Closed mouth: 16″ - $3,200.00, 19″ - $3,500.00, 25″ - $4,500.00
Marked F.G. on Gesland body with open mouth (two rows teeth): 15″ - $1,600.00, 18″ - $2,500.00, 26″ - $3,600.00

Plate 74 . . . . $3,900.00
Plate 75 . . . . $2,700.00
Plate 76 . . . . $3,400.00
Plate 77 . . . . $2,700.00
Plate 78 . . . . $4,300.00

Plate 79 .... $2,800.00
Plate 80 .... $1,800.00
Plate 81-82 .... $3,800.00
Plate 83 .... $2,400.00

Gesland

Plate 84 .... $5,900.00
Plate 85 .... $3,600.00
Plate 86 .... $3,400.00
Plate 87 .... $2,600.00
Plate 88 .... $4,000.00

Fortune Tellers

Fortune Telling Doll: open mouth, excellent condition with no cracks, hairlines and originally dressed: 12″ - $900.00+, 16″ - $1,400.00+, 20″ - $1,800.00+, 24″ - $2,400.00+

Plate 89 .... $2,000.00+
Plate 90 .... $2,000.00+

Fouquet & Douville

Plate 91 .... 18″ $2,800.00
Plate 91 .... 20″ $3,000.00
Plate 91 .... 26″ $3,900.00

H

The quality can differ greatly with these dolls, and the highest prices are paid for the perfect, beautiful examples only. Closed mouth, no damage and nicely dressed:

Excellent quality: 16″ - $18,000.00, 20″ - $26,000.00, 25″ - $30,000.00
Moderate or less quality to artist work: 16″ - $8,000.00, 20″ - $9,500.00, 25″ - $14,000.00

Plate 92-93 .... $27,000.00

H.G.

Closed mouth, original or nicely redressed, undamaged: 16″ - $4,600.00, 20″ - $8,200.00, 25″ - $12,500.00
Open mouth, original or nicely redressed and undamaged: 16″ - $2,400.00, 20″ - $4,000.00, 25″ - $5,200.00

Plate 94 .... $12,500.00
Plate 95 .... close-up

Jullien

Child doll: closed mouth. Jullien dolls can be excellent quality and many are not pretty dolls and may have poor quality of painting and/or bisque: Prices are for excellent quality dolls and others will be less. No damage and nicely dressed: 18″ - $3,200.00, 20″ - $3,500.00, 24″ - $3,900.00, 28″ - $4,800.00

Open mouth, excellent quality, no damage and nicely dressed: 18″ - $1,800.00, 20″ - $2,000.00, 24″ - $2,400.00, 28″ - $2,700.00

Plate 96 .... $3,400.00
Plate 97 .... $2,200.00

Jumeau

Tété Jumeau: Closed mouth with larger sizes having applied ears. No damage, nicely dressed: 10″ - $3,200.00, 12″ - $2,200.00, 14″ - $2,300.00, 16″ - $2,600.00, 19″ - $3,000.00, 21″ - $3,400.00, 23″ - $3,800.00, 25″ - $3,900.00, 28″ - $4,500.00, 30″ - $5,500.00
Tété Jumeau. Open mouth, nicely dressed and no damage: 10″ - $995.00, 12″ - $1,400.00, 14″ - , 16″ - $1,600.00, 19″ - $1,900.00, 21″ - $2,100.00, 23″ - $2,300.00, 25″ - $2,500.00, 28″ - $2,800.00, 30″ - $3,000.00
1907 - Jumeau. Incised 1907 and sometimes has Tété Jumeau stamp. Sleep or set eyes, no damage and nicely dressed. Open mouth: 14″ - $1,100.00, 17″ - $1,500.00, 20″ - $1,800.00, 25″ - $2,300.00, 28″ - $2,800.00, 32″ - $3,200.00
E.J. Child: Incised: Depose E.J. Closed mouth, unjointed wrists, no damage and very nicely dressed: 10″ - $4,500.00, 14″ - $5,200.00, 16″ - $5,700.00, 19″ - $6,200.00, 21″ - $7,500.00
Déposé Jumeau. Incised mark. Closed mouth, correct body with unjointed wrists, no damage and nicely dressed: 15″ - $4,800.00, 18″ - $5,000.00, 22″ - $5,700.00, 25″ - $6,400.00
Long Face "Cody" Jumeau. Closed mouth, straight wrists, size number on head, marked Jumeau body. No damage and nicely dressed: 20-21″ - $14,000+, 29-30″ - $20,000.00+
Portrait Jumeau: Closed mouth, usually has large almond-shaped eyes, straight wrists. Head marked with size number and body marked with Jumeau label. No damage and nicely dressed: 12″ - $4,200.00, 16″ - $5,200.00, 20″ - $6,200.00, 24″ - $7,000.00
Phonograph in Jumeau body: Open mouth, no damage, working and nicely dressed: 20″ - $3,400.00+, 25″ - $4,800.00+
Wire eye: Flirty eyes with lever in back of head to operate eyes, open mouth, no damage and nicely dressed: 20″ - $5,500.00, 24″ - $6,000.00
Celluloid head marked Jumeau: 14″ - $495.00
Two faced Jumeau. Has two different faces with one crying and other smiling. Open/closed mouths, jointed body. No damage and nicely dressed: 14″ - $7,800.00+
Fashion: See Fashion section.
DEP. mark: See DEP section.
Composition body lady: Marked Tété Jumeau on head, adult body, no damage and beautifully dressed: 18″ - $4,800.00, 21″ - $5,400.00
Mold 221: 10″ small dolls with paper sticker on clothes: Jumeau Adult style faces with closed

mouths and glass eyes. Bisque head on jointed body. Dressed in original ornate long gowns, no damage: 10″ - $500.00

Princess Elizabeth Mold 306: Jumeau made after formation of Unis and marked: Unis/France in oval with 71 on one side and 149 on other, followed by 306/Jumeau/1938/Paris. Closed mouth, paperweight or flirty eyes, jointed body, no damage and nicely dressed: 20″ - $1,400.00, 30″ - $2,200

S.F.B.J. or Unis: Marked along with Jumeau. Open mouth, no damage and nicely dressed: 16″ - $900.00, 20″ - $1,200.00

Plate 98 . . . . $6,400.00
Plate 99 . . . . $5,200.00
Plate 100 . . . . $5,400.00
Plate 101 . . . . $4,000.00-5,000.00
Plate 102 . . . . $9,600.00
Plate 103 . . . . side view
Plate 104 . . . . $5,000.00
Plate 105 . . . . $3,200.00
Plate 106 . . . . NPA
Plate 107 . . . . $18,000.00
Plate 108 . . . . $7,400.00
Plate 109 . . . . $16,000.00
Plate 110 . . . . $14,000.00
Plate 111 . . . . $3,400.00
Plate 112 . . . . $16,000.00
Plate 113-114 . . . . $16,000.00
Plate 115 . . . . $3,200.00
Plate 116 . . . . $3,200.00
Plate 117 . . . . $3,200.00
Plate 118 . . . . $3,000.00
Plate 119 . . . . 18″ body only - $500.00+
Plate 120 . . . . $5,600.00
Plate 121 . . . . $6,400.00
Plate 122 . . . . $3,000.00
Plate 123 . . . . $3,800.00
Plate 124 . . . . $3,200.00
Plate 125 . . . . $6,000.00
Plate 126 . . . . $6,000.00
Plate 127 . . . . $6,400.00
Plate 128 . . . . $2,000.00
Plate 129 . . . . $3,200.00
Plate 130 . . . . $2,200.00
Plate 131 . . . . $2,500.00
Plate 132 . . . . $1,800.00
Plate 133 . . . . $2,200.00
Plate 134 . . . . $5,200.00
Plate 135 . . . . $2,400.00
Plate 136 . . . . $7,000.00
Plate 137 . . . . $500.00
Plate 138 . . . . $3,200.00
Plate 139 . . . . $1,600.00+
Plate 140 . . . . $800.00
Plate 141 . . . . $2,600.00+

Lejeune

Plate 142 . . . . $3,200.00

Limoges

Child Doll: Open mouth, set eyes, on jointed body. No damage and nicely dressed. Good quality bisque with pretty face: 16″ - $650.00, 20″ - $800.00, 23″ - $900.00, 26″ - $1,100.00

Poor quality bisque with very high coloring or blotchy colored bisque: 16″ - $400.00, 20″ - $475.00, 23″ - $525.00, 26″ - $645.00

Character: Open/closed mouth with teeth, smiling fat face, glass eyes, on jointed body and not damaged. Nicely dressed. Marked: TOTO: 16″ - $700.00, 18″ - $1,000.00, 22″ - $1,200.00

Lady: Adult looking face, set eyes, open/closed mouth or full closed mouth and on jointed adult body. No damage and correctly dressed: 14″ - $550.00, 16-17″ - $900.00

Plate 143 . . . . $1,300.00
Plate 144 . . . . $550.00
Plate 145 . . . . $600.00
Plate 146 . . . . $800.00+
Plate 147 . . . . $800.00+
Plate 148 . . . . $550.00
Plate 149 . . . . $850.00
Plate 150 . . . . $475.00
Plate 151 . . . . $475.00

Mascotte

Some of the dolls are marked: Bébé Mascotte/Paris and others with an incised M and a number. No damage and nicely dressed: Closed mouth: 16″ - $3,000.00, 18″ - $3,400.00, 20″ - $3,800.00, 22″ - $4,200.00, 24″ - $4,500.00, 30″ - $6,000.00

Plate 152 . . . . $3,000.00
Plate 153 . . . . $4,000.00

Mechanical

Plate 154-155 . . . . NPA
Plate 156 . . . . $1,400.00+
Plate 157 . . . . $3,800.00+
Plate 158 . . . . $3,800.00+
Plate 159 . . . . $1,600.00+
Plate 160 . . . . $1,600.00+
Plate 161 . . . . $6,000.00+
Plate 162 . . . . $6,000.00+
Plate 163 . . . . $3,800.00+
Plate 164 . . . . NPA
Plate 165 . . . . $1,800.00+

Mothereau

Plate 166 . . . . $18,000.00+

Pannier

Plate 167 . . . . $2,000.00
Plate 168 . . . . close-up

Papier Mache

Plate 169 . . . . $1,200.00+
Plate 170 . . . . $1,000.00+

Paris Bébé

Child: Closed mouth, glass eyes, jointed body, no damage and nicely dressed: 16″ - $1,700.00, 20″ - $2,800.00, 24″ - $4,200.00, 26″ - $4,600.00

Plate 171 .... $4,000.00
Plate 172 .... $1,000.00
Plate 173 .... $4,000.00
Plate 174 .... $4,000.00

Phenix

Marked Phenix Bébé with French jointed body that may have one-piece arms and legs, closed mouth, no damage and well dressed: 16″ - $2,600.00, 22″ - $3,500.00, 25″ - $4,200.00. Same as above but with open mouth: 16″ - $1,400.00, 20″ - $1,900.00, 25″ - $2,800.00

Plate 175 .... $3,400.00+
Plate 176 .... $3,500.00+
Plate 177 .... $3,400.00+

R.D.

Child: Closed mouth, pretty face, jointed body, no damage and nicely dressed: 14″ - $1,700.00, 17″ - $2,400.00, 20″ - $2,700.00, 22″ - $3,000.00, 25″ - $3,500.00.

Child: with open mouth, no damage and nicely dressed: 17″ - $1,600.00, 20″ - $1,900.00, 22″ - $2,000.00

Plate 178 .... $1,800.00
Plate 179 .... $3,700.00
Plate 180 .... $1,900.00+
Plate 181 .... $2,400.00
Plate 182 .... $2,200.00
Plate 183 .... $1,800.00

Schmitt & Fils

Child: Bisque head on jointed composition/wood body with closed or open/closed mouth. No damage, nicely dressed: 15″ - $5,800.00, 18″ - $7,200.00, 20″ - $8,000.00, 23″ - $10,000.00, 25″ - $12,000.00

Plate 184 .... $4,000.00
Plate 185 .... close-up
Plate 186 .... $10,000.00
Plate 187 .... $6,000.00
Plate 188 .... $10,000.00
Plate 189 .... $11,000.00

S.F.B.J.

Child: Sleep or set eyes, open mouth, jointed body and nice face color. No damage and nicely dressed: Mold #60: 14″ - $465.00, 20″ - $600.00, 24″ - $750.00.

Same as above only mold #301: 8″ - $200.00, 14″ - $650.00, 18″ - $750.00, 22″ - $875.00, 28″ - $1,200.00, 32″ - $1,800.00

Jumeau type: 16″ - $900.00, 20″ - $1,250.00, 24″ - $1,600.00, 28″ - $2,800.00

Closed mouth: 16″ - $1,200.00, 20″ - $1,600.00, 24″ - $2,000.00, 28″ - $2,400.00.

Character: Sleep or set eyes, wigged or molded hair and some may have flocked hair over molded. Composition body. No damage and nicely dressed:

Mold #211: 16″ - $4,700.00
Mold #226: 16″ - $1,800.00, 21″ - $2,500.00
#227: 16″ - $1,800.00, 21″ - $2,600.00
#230: 23″ - $1,900.00
#233: 14″ - $2,500.00, 17″ - $3,600.00
#234: 16″ - $2,700.00, 21″ - $3,200.00
#235: 16″ - $1,800.00, 21″ - $2,500.00
#236 Toddlers: 12″ - $1,300.00, 16″ - $1,600.00, 20″ - $2,000.00, 25″ - $2,300.00
#236 Baby: 16″ - $1,200.00, 21″ - $1,600.00
#237: 16″ - $1,800.00, 21″ - $2,000.00
#238: 16″ - $2,600.00, 21″ - $3,000.00
#238 Lady: 24″ - $3,900.00
#239 (Poubout) 14″ - $16,000.00, 17″ - $19,000.00
#242: 17″ - $4,200.00
#247: 16″ - $2,300.00, 21″ - $2,800.00
#251 Toddler: 16″ - $1,300.00, 20″ - $1,900.00, 26″ - $2,600.00
#251 Baby: 10″ - 1,000.00; 16″ - $1,600.00, 21″ - $2,000.00
#252 Toddler: 16″ - $4,500.00, 20″ - $7,000.00, 26″ - $8,500.00
#252 Baby: 10″ - $2,000.00, 16″ - $2,400.00
#257: 16″ - $2,000.00
#266: 20″ - $1,900.00

Googly: Mold #245: No damage and nicely dressed: 14-15″ - $5,000.00

Kissing, talking and walking doll: Composition body with straight legs, walking mechanism and when walks, arms go up and throws a kiss. Head moves from side to side. Flirty eyes and open mouth. Prices are for dolls in working condition, no damage and nicely dressed: 21-22″- $1,600.00

Plate 190 .... $1,500.00
Plate 191 .... $2,000.00
Plate 192 .... $700.00
Plate 193 .... $1,300.00
Plate 194 .... $3,200.00
Plate 195 .... $550.00
Plate 196
#226 .... $1,400.00
#227 .... $1,700.00
#233 .... $3,400.00
Plate 197 .... $2,800.00
Plate 198 .... $1,500.00
Plate 199 .... $7,000.00
Plate 200 .... $1,600.00
Plate 201 .... $700.00
Plate 202 .... $465.00
Plate 203 .... $800.00
Plate 204 .... $300.00
#251 .... $1,000.00
Plate 205 .... NPA

Plate 206
16″ $3,500.00
18″ $1,500.00
22″ $4,200.00
Plate 207 .... $465.00
Plate 208 .... $1,500.00
Plate 209
18″ F.G. $3,200.00
18″ #236 .... $1,800.00
18″ #238 .... $2,900.00
19″ Steiner $4,400.00
19″ Unknown $4,200.00
21″ #247 .... $2,800.00
Plate 210
15″ SFBJ $650.00
15″ #226 .... $1,700.00
15″ #227 .... $1,700.00

Steiner, Jules

"A" Series Steiner Child: Closed mouth, jointed body, no damage and nicely dressed: 12″ - $2,300.00, 16″ - $3,400.00, 20″ - $4,500.00, 25″ - $5,000.00, 28″ - $6,800.00

"A" Series, same as above, but open mouth: 16″ - $1,400.00, 20″ - $2,500.00, 25″ - $3,600.00

Bourgoin Steiner: Closed mouth, jointed body, no damage and nicely dressed: 16″ - $3,800.00, 20″ - $4,500.00, 25″ - $5,000.00

Wire Eye Steiner: Closed mouth, flat glass eyes that open and close by moving a wire that comes out the back of head. Jointed body, no damage and nicely dressed: Bourgon: 16″ - $3,800.00, 20″ - $4,600.00, 25″ - $5,200.00.

"C" Series Steiner with wire eyes: 16″ - $3,600.00, 20″ - $4,600.00, 25″ - $5,400.00

"A" Series with wire eyes: 16″ - $4,000.00, 20″ - $4,800.00, 25″ - $5,600.00

"C" Series Steiner: Closed mouth, jointed body, no damage and nicely dressed: 16″ - $3,600.00, 20″ - $4,600.00, 25″ - $5,400.00

Mechanical Steiner: Key wound, kicks and cries, moves head, open mouth with two rows of teeth. In working order, not damaged and nicely dressed: 18″ - $1,800.00

Bisque hip Steiner: Motchmann style body with bisque head, shoulders, lowers arms, and legs, and bisque torso section. No damage anywhere and nicely dressed: 18″ - $4,400.00+

Pink wash over eyes, on jointed Steiner body. No damage, nicely dressed: 14″ - $1,200.00, 18″ - $2,600.00

Plate 211 .... $4,700.00
Plate 212 .... $2,800.00
Plate 213 .... $5,600.00
Plate 214-217 .... NPA
Plate 218 .... $5,000.00
Plate 219 .... $4,300.00
Plate 220 .... $4,500.00
Plate 221 .... $3,700.00
Plate 222 .... $4,000.00
Plate 223 .... $4,800.00
Plate 224 .... $3,500.00
Plate 225 .... $4,700.00
Plate 226 .... $1,900.00+
Plate 227
18″ Belton $1,900.00
18″ Bru Jne $9,000.00
19″ A Series $4,400.00

Unknown

Plate 228 .... $4,400.00
Plate 229 .... $2,600.00+
Plate 230 .... $1,800.00
Plate 231 .... $4,200.00
Plate 232 .... $2,600.00+
Plate 233 .... $2,000.00
Plate 234 .... $2,900.00
Plate 235 .... $1,900.00
Plate 236-237 .... $5,000.00

Unis

#60,70,71,301: Bisque head with papier mache or composition jointed body. Sleep or set eyes, open mouth, not damaged and nicely dressed: 14″ - $450.00, 17″ - $525.00, 21″ - $650.00, 24″ - $750.00

Black or Brown: 14″ - $525.00, 17″ - $600.00

Provincial Costume doll: Bisque head, painted, set or sleep eyes, open mouth (or closed on smaller dolls). Five piece body. Original Provincial costume, No damage and in very good condition: 6″ - $175.00, 12″ - $265.00, 14″ - $295.00

Black or Brown: 6″ - $200.00, 12″ - $325.00, 14″ - $385.00

On fully jointed body: 12″ - $300.00, 14″ - $365.00

Baby: Mold #272, glass eyes, wide open mouth: 14″ - $400.00, 17″ - $800.00

Plate 238 .... $485.00
Plate 239 .... $950.00

Other Books by Patricia Smith

Modern Collector's Dolls I, Hardbound #1079 .... $17.95
Modern Collector's Dolls II, Hardbound #1080 .... $17.95
Modern Collector's Dolls III, Hardbound #1081 .... $17.95
Modern Collector's Dolls IV, Hardbound #1082 .... $17.95
Modern Collector's Dolls V, Hardbound #1516 .... $19.95

Patricia Smith's Doll Values, Antique to Modern IV, Paperback #1683 .... $9.95
Patricia Smith's Doll Values, Antique to Modern V, Paperback, color #1815 .... $9.95

Madame Alexander Collector's Dolls Hardbound #1067 .... $19.95
Madame Alexander Collector's Dolls II Hardbound #1068 .... $19.95
Madame Alexander Price Guide 14 (free with above two books) Paperback #1840 .... $4.95
World of Alexanderkins Hardbound, color #1648 .... $19.95

German Dolls Paperback, color #1631 .... $9.95
Vogue Ginny Dolls Hardbound, color #1630 .... $19.95